FULLY COMPLIANT & CONSCIENTIOUS

STRAIGHT TALK ABOUT HOW TO DO THINGS IN BUSINESS RIGHT!

DR. AMIT DAS

Made with ♥ on the Notion Press Platform
www.notionpress.com

To

All my bosses and mentors who made a difference in my professional career.

"Organisations throughout the world are still being harmed and brought down by systematic noncompliance or the sins of a few, and the media are full of stories about corporate scandals and crimes. Investors, lawmakers, and regulators are putting pressure on multinational organisations to enhance their corporate governance, business sustainability, and corporate culture in today's economic climate. Employees and decision-makers need clear, detailed, and practical compliance information to help their organisations prosper and thrive. "

- Dr. Amit Das, Motivational Speaker, Leadership Coach , Counsellor, and Mentor.

Contents

Foreword

"An organisation that lacks ethical standards will not exist for long. In business, your business compliance and conscientiousness are what distinguish you. This will influence how your consumers and employees see your organisation's existence."

Dear Reader,

This book offers cutting-edge content, including both creative and fresh, thought-provoking topics, with a focus on integrating conscientiousness into practical compliance management. This book, **"Fully Compliant & Conscientious,"** is the most reader-friendly text on the business since it takes a complete, realistic, inventive, and practical approach to business ethical practices. The author, Dr. Amit Das, connects the multiple facets of employees' behaviour to business compliance in their work, illustrating how fully compliant behaviour and conscientiousness may be used together to create a holistic learning environment. This book is a thorough foundation for comprehending the most pressing global business concerns, including business sustainability, corporate social responsibilities, and organisational ombudsman. This book will guide you through the process of honing the critical thinking and analytical abilities you'll need to tackle the particular set of issues that arise when ethics and commerce intersect.

This book, **"Fully Compliant & Conscientious,"** educates business executives, students, and other readers on how to recognise these unethical traps, avoid them, and dig their way out if they do fall into them. The author outlines some of the behaviours and expectations that may be implemented immediately in your organisation to encourage ethical conduct from the top down. The author also shows ethics in action, such as how to cope with circumstances where the correct solution isn't obvious. The following business ethics objectives will be met by reading this book: ethical decision-making, deliberate blindness, individual ethics at work, ethical leadership, unethical behaviour at work, and a method for dealing with unethical concerns. Author's examples give fantastic role-playing opportunities and possibilities to improve your grasp of soft skills like communication, persuasion, presentation, leadership, and a global attitude.

This book, **"Fully Compliant & Conscientious,"** is a comprehensive yet approachable examination of the key ethical theories and how they relate to the primary stakeholders confronted with this issue. The author of this book succeeded in explaining precisely, pleasantly, and in an easily understandable way what everybody should know and do in compliance and conscientious. This book uses a flexible modular approach to shed light on modern corporate challenges by providing a full description of the corporate governance process and the many motivations within today's governance system, as well as prospective solutions in context.

This book provides clear, detailed, and practical information for practitioners and decision-makers in any organisation or corporation. It describes in layman's words the skills, tools, and attitude required to build and deliver a best-practice compliance and ethics program—one that complies with legal, stakeholder, and societal standards and protects your organisation from fines, penalties, and reputational harm.

This book attempts to help organisation managers improve their ethical awareness and decision-making abilities, as well as address their issues. This book is intended not just for management students, but also as a resource for academics and professionals in the area. This book provides readers with a thorough overview of business ethics and corporate governance ideas. The necessity of ethical principles in addressing ethical challenges in today's highly dynamic corporate environment is emphasised in this book. It also goes into the corporate governance structure in great depth. Its components, as well as how it is implemented in India and overseas, numerous real-life examples offered in this book aid in the learning of ideas, and discussions centred on these instances provide a deeper grasp of real-world business procedures.

It will guide you through the process of honing the critical thinking and analytical abilities you'll need to tackle the particular set of issues that arise when ethics and commerce intersect. This book investigates why rules-based, tick-box, defended compliance continues to fail, and proposes a new strategy for businesses that want to thrive and prosper. The author of this book has succeeded in expressing what everyone should know and do in terms of compliance and ethics in a should be complimented for his approach to producing a book that every professional should read. The author, Dr. Amit Das, gives the depth of knowledge required to assist organisations in navigating ethics and compliance in an effective and integrated manner.

The misconception that governance, risk management, and compliance are minor considerations in the inner workings ofan organisation is refuted. In reality, it is the success of these efforts that contributes to total market gains, with the high-profile failures of huge banking institutions, large oil organisations, and real estate used to demonstrate the point.

This book provides cutting-edge material, including innovative and unusual study aids as well as fresh, thought-provoking content, with an emphasis on integrating corporate governance into practical management. The authors' contribution to sensitizing diverse stakeholders of contemporary organisations on corporate governance, corporate social responsibility, and business ethics in general.

This book's entertaining tone will take its readers beyond the word "compliance," which is perceived as so negative by many, and illustrate how to win hearts and minds. Telling tales is a practical and beneficial technique to make learning more memorable and effective. The author deserve praise for his innovative approach to providing a must-read for every professional and student. For those teaching business ethics at universities and business schools, this is a foundational management text.

This book addresses a vacuum in the literature on business ethics by using an overall interdisciplinary approach and merging new research results from fields like economics, business administration, behavioural economics, philosophy, psychology, and sociology. The book opens with a definition of business ethics, a description of its goals, and a discussion of the relevance of business ethics to companies, the economy, and society. This is a thorough and practical handbook that will assist you in dealing with real-life ethical difficulties that arise in the workplace.

This book gives the concepts needed to comprehend and effectively handle ethical dilemmas wherever you are in the world, thanks to a genuinely worldwide viewpoint and a variety of creative learning features. To get a better grasp of markets, business, and economic life, this book presents a study of ethics and values.

In examining what works and what doesn't, the book strikes the correct balance between ethics and values on the one hand and compliance program aspects on the other. It is well-written and easy to comprehend, and it offers useful information for both seasoned compliance professionals and newbies to the industry. It deftly incorporates real-world tales and anecdotes into the lessons in a fun way, bringing the debate to life. It is required reading for anyone on the compliance path and is destined to become a compliance literature classic.

This book is highly relevant for students and professionals today due to its coverage of the ethical theories underlying business and their application in the real world, as well as a special focus on ethical issues in consumer protection and the information technology sector, whistle-blowing, and real-life corporate incidents. This book is a thorough foundation for comprehending the most pressing global business concerns, including business sustainability, corporate governance, and organisational ethics, is available as an e-book.

This book covers a wide range of business ethics ideas and emphasises the role of ethical principles in resolving moral difficulties in the workplace. Dr. Amit Das brings out tiny but significant successes in reimagining a current compliance training program or building new courses across fully compliant platforms, which may transform sceptics into champions of learning. The book discusses how to engage employees in a way that inspires them while avoiding sanctions and reputational damage. The human component may be disregarded while formulating laws and regulations.

However, an effective compliance and ethical program relies heavily on the human component. It's not just about selecting people who will follow orders but also about engaging with them so that they will advocate business ideals.

Thank you for taking the time to learn more about business compliance and conscientiousness. Thank you for taking the time to read this book.

So, happy reading and learning to all my readers.

Carpe diem.

Dr. Amit Das

Leadership Coach , Counsellor, and Mentor.

Preface

"Trust in your products and services will grow as a result of good business compliance and conscientiousness. Many corporate executives now believe that their positions imply responsibilities for the well-being of the larger community. They do not see themselves as profit-making robots but as tools to meet the growing expectations of their consumers."

In the current corporate environment, ethics in business is a new dimension that has evolved internationally. Transparency, responsibility, and accountability not only increase consumer confidence but also raise employee morale. This is despite growing ethical expectations from stakeholders, the ability of social media to expose businesses, the proliferation of compliance rules and regulations, and the growing number of policies, processes, and compliance officers put in place in response. So, why is it that compliance isn't working?

This book, **"Fully Compliant & Conscientious,"** provides an overview and analysis of key developments in contemporary business ethics by looking at them in terms of their diachronic development – key thinkers, key issues, and key institutions, as well as how they all contributed to current understandings of business ethics, governance, and practise. This book explains how ethical beliefs help people persevere in difficult circumstances and flourish in the long run, using examples from a variety of enterprises, sectors, and nations.

"Corruption is nothing new, but as a culture, you're more aware of it and more willing to believe in changes."

The prevalent idea that there are inescapable trade-offs between performing morally and flourishing financially is debunked by real-world success tales. A simple and straightforward guide to ethical business practises based on common-sense moral concepts. This book, "**Fully Compliant & Conscientious,**" provides succinct solutions to the three most critical ethical problems faced by business professionals.

- What distinguishes good from bad business practises?
- Why do excellent, respectable entrepreneurs occasionally do the wrong thing?
- How can you utilise the answers to these questions to improve the behaviour of yourself, your coworkers, your supervisors, and your employees?

In business, poor behaviour is rarely the product of bad intentions. Most individuals have good intentions most of the time. In this book, **"Fully Compliant & Conscientious,"** I have investigated why rules-based, tick-box, defended compliance continues to fail, and proposes a new strategy for businesses that want to thrive and prosper. This book highlights the benefits that a really successful compliance and ethics programme can provide when it works hand in hand with a values-based culture of shared ownership, including competitive advantage, career happiness, employee and customer loyalty, and brand improvement. Corruption is nothing new, but as a culture, you're more aware of it and more willing to believe changes. Rather than brushing allegations under the floor or rejecting complaints, businesses are increasingly giving people who raise concerns a voice. However, you may be wondering what you can do to avoid corruption and unethical behaviour in the first place in your company.

This is a book for everyone who wants to learn how to increase employee engagement and motivation. This bookhighlights the benefits that a really effective compliance and ethics programme can provide when it works hand in hand with a values-based culture of shared ownership, including competitive advantage, career fulfilment, employee and customer loyalty, and brand improvement. This book, **"Fully Complaint & Conscientious,"** argues that the best compliance training programmes must be both practical and adaptable in order to modify employee behaviour and, as a result, reduce the likelihood of misbehaviour occurring in the first place. Only by balancing the demands of the employees with those of the organisation can compliance training be successful.

Compliance and conscientiousness are sometimes viewed as stringent sets of rules and procedures, making individuals fearful of deviating from the norm rather than fostering buy-in. This book questions this industry standard, portraying it as the reason why compliance is a faulty idea in business. It is beneficial because it paves the way for clear documentation and defensible measures for businesses that want to avoid any potential legal liabilities brought on by their employees. Focusing on the what and how without addressing why leads to an emotional connection and disengaged employees who are more likely to burn out.

This book will assist you in comprehending the crucial architecture that underpins every organisation's driving power. You'll discover how to avoid key errors by reading this book, as well as how to seize the proper opportunities for continuing company success. The book investigates why some great corporations have failed while others have thrived. I do emphasise the importance of compliance, ethics, and risk management practises in achieving success. I look at how the board of directors may oversee company strategy, CEO remuneration, succession planning, crisis management, performance assessment, board composition, and even shareholder communications.

Investors, lawmakers, and regulators are putting pressure on multinational organisations to enhance their corporate governance, business sustainability, and corporate culture in today's economic climate. This long-awaited work delves deep into each of these three critical areas, helping readers achieve a thorough understanding through features such as chapter summaries, key words, discussion questions.

"In today's global business climate, business sustainability, corporate governance, and organisational ethics are gaining centre stage."

It is vital to keep oneself up to date with in-depth knowledge in order to stay ahead of the competition. Any entrepreneur understands the value of acquiring such resources. It makes sense for a businessperson to have the most up-to-date business ethics book in their personal library, such as this one. This book stresses the real-world significance of crucial themes, including the essence of morality, main theories of ethics and economic justice, and contrasting perspectives on capitalism and corporate responsibility. It is comprehensive, adaptable, and designed to increase readers‘ engagement with the subject in order to improve their knowledge and understanding.

This bookis organised around interrelated layers of organisational behaviour, with an emphasis on ethics at the individual, group, and organisational levels. In addition to business realities, I would offer a critical perspective on how these things can only be accomplished by harmonising culture, strategy, compliance processes, and other perks like remuneration.

The misconception that governance, risk management, and compliance are minor considerations in the inner workings of an organisation is refuted. In reality, it is the success of these efforts that contributes to total market gains, with the high-profile failures of huge banking institutions, large oil organisations, and real estate used to demonstrate the point. Examples that depict real-life situations and allow readers to grapple with moral ambiguity. Students and professionals are challenged to see alternative moral views and practise ethical decision-making through reading this book. This short, well-organised work will be a great tool for students and professionals taking corporate ethics courses to comprehend ethics in the digital era.

"Ethics extends beyond the realm of business. In the long term, ethical business and marketing methods are sustainable."

Corporate business processes must be constantly improved, transparent, compassionate, truthful, and respectful. Such businesses set the bar for good corporate governance. Corporate corruption tales abound in today's news. These incidents are frequently blamed on top-level decision-makers, and properly so in most situations. Modern business executives are responsible for both promoting ethical conduct and dealing with ethical snafus that arise during their term.

I will discuss major ethical issues in this book. You have a responsibility to fulfil. That assumption is that you would conduct yourself in an ethical manner and represent your company as such. As a result, this is a very crucial discussion that you should have. I would like to offer a set of principles and things to think about in your debate so that you can go through that grey area with the best chance of coming up with a good, sound ethical solution.

People are where ethics may be found. In truth, the organisation's ethics are represented by its leaders. The majority of businesses have a set of codified ethical guidelines. And although that gives advice, which is wonderful, whatever conduct emanates from the organisation's executives symbolises the organisation's ethics. Whether you like it or not, you're representing a organisation.

In examining what works and what doesn't, the book strikes the correct balance between ethics and values on the one hand and compliance programme aspects on the other. It is well-written and easy to comprehend, and it offers useful information for both seasoned compliance professionals and newbies to the industry. It deftly incorporates real-world tales and anecdotes into the lessons in a fun way, bringing the debate to life. It is required reading for anyone on the compliance path.

In this instructive read, Dr. Amit Das challenges typical compliance training programmes in a number of thought-provoking ways. With a seemingly never-ending list of compliance concerns to handle, I believe that businesses should select learning programs that serve higher and broader goals, with the ultimate objective of fostering a resilient workplace culture that prioritises integrity and ethics.

Employees who are engaged are more inclined to be proud and ardent about supporting the corporate principles with which they agree. In summary, an optimistic attitude yields greater results than a fear-based strategy. A compliance and ethics program, when effectively implemented, transforms employees into stakeholders. An organisation's culture of shared ownership can be transformed by this values-based culture. It's not only about spreading good vibes. Compliance and ethics are great ways to set clear standards for workers and make it easier for them to understand how success is assessed. Providing honest, non-confrontational feedback to decision-makers in order to help employees thrive.

Clear expectations channelled toward good progress transform feedback into something to be desired rather than feared. This book lays the groundwork for this strategy. Rules can help establish expectations, but it's the culture of the organisation that makes it effective. This bookrecognises the delicate balance that must be achieved and offers a clear method to do so.

This book, "Fully Compliant & Conscientious," is a lively and entertaining introduction to the topic of corporate ethics. It provides practical counsel for handling ethical challenges in business, based on illustrative examples such as the Ford Pinto case, Enron, Walmart, and British Petroleum. presents readers with unsolved current case studies to ponder, encouraging them to participate in decision-making and make their own recommendations.

I believe that risk management should not be centred on what has occurred or the issues that need to be addressed. Instead, concentrate on prospective difficulties and how to be proactive when it comes to risk management. Once again I would like to remind the reader that senior management's actions are significantly more important in shaping organisational culture. I will explain how senior leaders may achieve their objectives by incorporating the proper organisation, processes, and technology. And how effective CEOs and directors shape, manage, and monitor their organisations in order to achieve these goals.

Rather than flying over abstract notions and philosophical discussions at the treetop level, this book assists professionals by taking them on a tour through the tough world of business ethics at the ground level of the corporation. Employees can have a better understanding of how their corporate code of ethics connects to operational decisions made on a daily basis by evaluating topics and scenarios that directly relate to their work environment.

Using this book, unique optimum ethical model, which defines how to select and educate ethical people, make ethical decisions, and establish a trustworthy, productive work environment, I will illustrate how to construct organisations that encourage ethical conduct and eliminate ethical hazards. This work takes a practical approach, with suggestions, techniques, and real-world examples focusing on a wide range of enterprises, sectors, and concerns.

Organisations such as Facebook, Google, Wells Fargo, Volkswagen, and Amazon are featured in a variety of real-world case studies. Slow and rapid thinking, the inherent tension between the individual and the organisation, conformity, and the problems of speaking the truth to power are all subjects treated in depth in this practical, down-to-earth text. As they wrestle with ethical challenges large and small, students and professionals are given abundant opportunities to participate in meaningful reflection, discussion, and application.

Students and professionals can practise their ethical reasoning skills through self-assessments, reflection features, and application projects. Through the prism of corporate compliance and strategy, this interesting book offers a fresh look at corporate bribery and corruption. It covers a wide range of topics, including regular corporate issues and bribery anecdotes, as well as examples of how unethical individuals invented unique bribery techniques. Corruption also draws attention to high-risk areas and industries, such as construction, healthcare, defence, and telecommunications. However, you should be aware that as you read this book, you may begin to suspect that no industry is truly devoid of bribery and corruption!

"Ethics is knowing the difference between what you have a right to do and what is right to do"- Potter Stewart

Making Ethical Decisions uses the weight-of-reasons method throughout the text to educate students on how to handle ethical dilemmas they may face. The goal of this decision-making framework is to solve ethical quandaries rather than to faithfully apply certain philosophical perspectives on what is good. Using this technique, I would like to give more stress on the need for employees at all levels to carefully consider the ethical consequences of their activities, and it may be implemented at the individual, organisational, and stakeholder levels. Each chapter includes a case that walks students through the framework's application, as well as mini-cases that allow students to experiment with the framework on their own.

This book investigates the function of moral ideals as economic productive forces as well as the impact of ethical and immoral behaviour on the economy. It demonstrates how ethics boosts economic production and gives particular ethics tools for students and managers to use. The book captures discussion of the relevance of ethics in the workplace and in the economy, as well as the ethics tools that management may use to encourage ethical behaviour among their employees.

I will discuss on how accounting has always been at the forefront of ethical challenges in business. This form of wrongdoing appears to be inescapable and must be reported in all cases. Today, the number one problem in every company is ethics in accounting processes. They falsify their income and spending in order to qualify for tax breaks. They falsify their financial figures to appear more prosperous. Owners of businesses are now individually scrutinizing their documents to ensure their correctness.

However, I believe that the epidemic has had an influence on this sort of ethical dilemma among corporations. People have been focused on purchasing basic things since there has been a noticeable reduction in consumption. As a result, they ignored elements that were not essential. With this, there are inclinations for organisations' advertising approaches to involve overpromising and misleading hopes in order to get customers to buy their goods. In times of crisis, it is unavoidable for enterprises to fight tooth and nail merely to stay in business.

This book is the first attempt to explain the circumstances that led to a focus on business ethics, particularly in the 2020-21 era, and how the broader field expanded to include related concepts like corporate governance, corporate social responsibility, ethical leadership, sustainable business, and responsible management education. However, your expectations for businesses are still shaped by an out-of-date mentality that prioritises shareholder profits over everything else. This book tells a fresh story about the nature of business, illustrating how today's most influential ideas and businesses are united by a commitment to responsibility and ethics.

It doesn't have to be a tough issue to discuss business ethics. Effective decision-making, policy development, and organisational management all hinge on a thorough grasp of the concepts that govern our daily lives. Explore the topic of corporate ethics via theory and examples from popular culture in this book. Learn how to properly negotiate the complex organisational morality of today's world with these practical recommendations. You all slip into moral quagmires without even realising it.

This book provides clear, detailed, and practical information for practitioners and decision-makers in any organisation or corporation. It describes, in layman's words, the skills, tools, and attitude required to build and deliver a best-practice compliance and ethics program—one that complies with legal, stakeholder, and societal standards and protects your company from fines, penalties, and reputational harm. You'll need to understand how to employ ethical methods, make ethical judgments, and include the most up-to-date knowledge on ethics and governance scandals, legal liabilities, and professional accounting and auditing difficulties. To sustain stakeholder support and for auditors to examine financial statements, you must understand why building an ethical business culture is critical.

"The misconception that governance, risk management, and compliance are minor considerations in the inner workings of an organisation is refuted. In reality, it is the success of these efforts that contributes to total market gains, with the high-profile failures of huge banking institutions, large oil organisations, and real estate used to demonstrate the point."

- Dr. Amit Das, Motivational Speaker, Leadership Coach , Counsellor, and Mentor.

Acknowledgements

At the outset, I will thank my family for supporting me throughout the journey of writing my book and encouraging me to live my dreams; my son has always been instrumental in giving his inspiration to complete the writing of this book. Despite the fact that I am listed as the author of this book, **"FULLY COMPLIANT & CONSCIENTIOUS,"** *would not have been published if I had depended entirely on my own talents. Creating this book required more than anything—it took a family of dedicated and caring people who were always prepared to lend a hand.*

Writing a book while working full-time is no simple task, so I'd want to express my gratitude to my amazing coworkers who act as cheerleaders in equal measure. Thank you, too, to my students and clients for your patience and unflinching support while I worked on this book!

Thank you to everyone who has listened to me argue for doing everything you can to make your life, including your work life, more progressive. I appreciate everyone's assistance throughout the process. This book would not have been possible without each of you having had an impact on my life in some manner.

Lastly, I would like to thank all the people with whom I have been associated. You gave me power. I would like to thank Notion Press for publishing my book. Finally, thank you all for gifting your time to read this book.

I'd want to convey my heartfelt appreciation to the almighty God for bestowing his blessings and being so gracious.

CHAPTER ONE

Business Ethics Can Not Be Reduced To Compliance

"Apart from values and ethics which I have tried to live by, the legacy I would like to leave behind is a very simple one - that I have always stood up for what I consider to be the right thing, and I have tried to be as fair and equitable as I could be." -Ratan Tata

We live in a time where the line between right and wrong is becoming increasingly blurred, and individual judgments have never been more subjective. Businesses are struggling to prosper, competition is rampant, and financial and celebrity achievement is more difficult to come by because our marketplaces are congested and competitive. The business ethics movement has yet to persuade many individuals. There is a lot of evidence that unethical behaviour may harman organisation's reputation and cause its stock price to drop.

Furthermore, ethical businesses are more likely to create trust among your shareholders, workers, customers, and the general public, which is obviously beneficial to your bottom line. Given the ever-changing and difficult business VUCCAD (Volatility, Uncertainty, Complexity, Conflict, Ambiguity, and Dynamism) landscape, making a profit is no longer the sole goal of running an organisation. Instead of reciprocating in a caring community, the environment has become a corporate need for long-term survival in this competitive world. Remember that in order to survive and develop in this competitive market, businesses must have solid corporate governance and adhere to all company regulations.

Nowadays, the terms "ethical" and "sustainable" are frequently used in conjunction with discussions about branding and marketing. Consumers perceive brands as more trustworthy, reliable, and compassionate towards your larger community or society when you embrace superior principles, tactics, and activities. As a result, company owners should always assess the strength of their marketing methods as well as whether or not their image goes far enough to make a difference or look valuable to society. An organisation that practises ethical marketing is more likely to instil a feeling of purpose in both its customers and employees.

What is the distinction between compliance and ethics?

I've witnessed considerable misunderstanding concerning the responsibilities of ethics and compliance in corporations. The way these two fields are identified contributes to the misunderstanding. Few organisations just have a compliance department, others have a department of compliance and conscientiouness . Some businesses employ a distinct chief ethics officer for compliance. To gain a better understanding of these critical positions, I asked multiple executives involved in both ethics and compliance to discuss the parallels and contrasts they found. I'll give various points of view, add my own perspective, and then evaluate what this implies for your career and your company.

Company values are similar to fingerprints. No two organisations' ideals and ethics are precisely the same. However, if you look at enough organisations, you'll notice some patterns develop. Some values and ethics are more prevalent than others. So I did precisely that in preparation for this book. I examined dozens of businesses to see which principles and ethics are most prevalent. Here's what I discovered. To begin with, when most people think about organisational values, the first thing that comes to mind is ethics, or doing what is right. That includes things like honesty, justice, transparency, and respect for all persons.

However, ethics is only one sort of value. Other forms of values show what individuals in an organisation want to accomplish and how they want to do it. That is why, regardless of the outcomes desired by the business, obtaining results is nearly always a stated or tacit organisational value. However, additional shared values concern how such outcomes are delivered. For example, many organisations prioritise leadership, discipline, and safety while striving for those outcomes, but others value having a passion for winning, cooperation, and even having fun along the road, or even all of those things. The interests of the individuals who are affected by the oragnisation's success or failure are the final but not least set of items that organisations value.

In reality, the quandary should be evident by now. With so many distinct things to value, it's easy to see how some of them can periodically clash with others, and that's when you'll discover out what your true values are. Before you begin with the first case, research and become acquainted with your company's principles and ethics.

What exactly is compliance?

The act of adhering to corporate rules and processes as required by laws and regulations is known as compliance. Compliance is a given. It entails adhering to the laws and regulations that govern your organisation's operations. Compliance is a framework for ensuring that an organisation and its workers comply with applicable rules and regulations while reducing the risk of noncompliance.

Compliance is a separate department responsible for identifying and managing risks such as sanctions and fines, financial losses, and reputational concerns. It is a critical foundation of any company's operation and culture, and it should be founded on the concepts of openness, impartiality, responsibility, integrity, professionalism, and ethics. Corporate compliance is the endeavour to avoid, detect, and correct legal and ethical difficulties. Compliance means following all of the regulations all of the time. When it came to ethics, the perspectives of these leaders ranged little.

What exactly is ethics?

The opportunity to participate, influence, and lead through the discipline of doing what is right is defined as ethics. Ethics go beyond what the law mandates. It entails doing the right thing and adhering to both the text and the spirit of the law. Because it requires adhering to one's personal code of behaviour, ethics is more difficult to describe than compliance. Everyone has their own set of morals. There is no such thing as a general guideline for ethics. But, at its core, ethics is about doing the right thing. Ethics refers to high-level principles and behavioural norms for doing the right thing. We educate ethics to help people make ethical decisions, both inside and outside of the established rules. Behaving ethically means acting in accordance with ideals such as respect, trust, and honesty.

The biggest financial crisis in history, as well as the atrocious fraud, greed, and corruption that led to it, harmed not only the banking industry, but companies and individuals all across the world. It might have been avoided simply if optimal business procedures had been followed. For the past few years, my team and I have been exploring multiple key areas of focus: corporate ethics, governing policies, ethical leadership, employees loyalty, organisational ombudsman, corporate conscientiousness, CSR, and whistleblowing. My purpose was to look at the best and worst management methods in these areas.

People are where ethics may be found. In truth, the organisation's ethics are represented by its leaders. The majority of businesses have a set of codified ethical guidelines. And although that gives advice, which is wonderful, whatever conduct emanates from the organisation's executives symbolises the organisation's ethics. Whether you like it or not, you're representing an organisation. I have set some priorities which include: prioritising purpose above profit; producing value for stakeholders over shareholders; viewing business as anchored in society rather than markets; acknowledging people's complete humanity as well as their economic interests; and combining business and ethics into a more holistic approach.

This year, nearly every organisation in the world was compelled to rethink their marketing strategies in order to suit a market ravaged by the COVID-19-20 epidemic. Many businesses opted to do so by leading with their principles, acknowledging their consumers' issues, and guiding their approach with empathy. So, the bottom line is that organisations that lead with a conscience are considerably more likely to be credited, trusted, and supported, which means that a values-driven approach is one of the most significant methods for brands to build a responsible marketing strategy.

In general, all of the descriptions above agree that ethics is concerned with right and wrong behavior. The basic components of such concepts differ slightly. We notice some major differences when they discuss the link between ethics and compliance. It is possible to be compliant without being ethical. We aim for both. We want to do what is right because it is the correct thing to do. By doing the right thing and following all of the regulations for compliance, you will not only be doing the right thing by your customers and consumers, but you will also avoid being hit with any type of enforcement action that will hinder you from doing what you want with your business. If banks are found to be in violation of different rules and regulations, they may face fines. Some of these penalties include not being allowed to create another branch or to purchase another organisation until you've cleared up whatever your compliance concerns are. We don't want to be in that circumstance, so the simplest way to avoid being in that situation is to be cooperative.

Unlike past generations of consumers, today's generation is considerably more interested in learning about the companies they support. This involves understanding what their goods are composed of, who manufactures them, and the ethical framework that binds them together, as well as their general practises, environmental imprint, and other factors. If you want to "do the right thing" in business, you must first determine why you're doing what you're doing and what your desired objective is. Is it to win, appear good, or even wipe out the competition? Is it to redefine greatness, highlight outstanding abilities, or effect good change? Are you attempting to prove or exhibit who you are? The former will promote egotistical banter, but the latter will produce togetherness, pride, and exceptional performance.

"Business ethics is successful when human resources are used effectively and efficiently."

You're setting yourself and your employees up for failure if you think you can transform the culture of your department or business overnight. Instead, conceive large, strategic concepts and then put them into action in little, tactical, step-by-step, incremental steps. Sure, you're focusing on cultures that promote ethics, compliance, and accountability, but this strategy is essential for any culture change project.

Every day, corporations face difficult decisions about the right thing to do, but how can a business act ethically as an organisation made up of individuals with diverse opinions and values?

Organisations continue to be harmed and taken down across the world as a result of systematic noncompliance or the sins of a few, and the media are full of stories of corporate scandals and crimes. This is despite growing ethical expectations from stakeholders, the ability of social media to expose businesses, the proliferation of compliance rules and regulations, and the growing number of policies, processes, and compliance officers put in place in response. So, why is it that compliance isn't working?

A notorious example of this was the 2001 Enron affair, in which the American energy company was exposed for years of falsely reporting its financial accounts, with its accounting firm, Arthur Andersen, signing off on numbers that were erroneous. The misrepresentation had an impact on stockholder prices, and public stockholders lost more than $25 billion as a result of this ethical infringement. Both organisations subsequently went out of business, and despite the fact that just a tiny part of the accounting firm's workers worked for Enron, the firm's demise resulted in the loss of 85,000 jobs.

Corporate corruption tales abound in today's news. These accidents are frequently blamed on top-level decision-makers, and properly so in most situations. Modern business executives are responsible for both promoting ethical conduct and dealing with ethical snafus that arise during their term. You have a responsibility to fulfil. That assumption is that you would conduct yourself in an ethical manner and represent your company as such.

As a result, this is a very crucial discussion that you should have. I would like to offer a set of principles and things to consider in your conversation so that you can go through that grey region with the best chance of success. And I would like to offer a set of principles and things to think about in your debate so that you can go through that grey area with the best chance of coming up with a good, sound ethical solution.

People are becoming increasingly aware of how you act as individuals and as corporations. If you act honestly, you'll have a solid reputation in the marketplace. If you don't behave ethically, you risk alienating the very individuals to whom you should be selling your goods. It would be so simple if ethics were a one-size-fits-all scenario. If you had to write and provide incorrect responses all of the time, One might be compared to the other. Go home, secure in the knowledge that you did the right thing. That is just not the case. In your respective nations, you have diverse cultures. Within a corporation, there are diverse cultures, and even within a country, there are different expectations.

Knowing the standards for where you are at the moment is crucial to understanding how you should act ethically or what defines ethical action. So there you have it: your company's culture. There's your country's culture. There are the laws in your own nation. From an ethical standpoint, there are the standards you've set, and being consistent in how you deal with your peers, customers, and management team to extend the idea of one size doesn't fit all from an ethical standpoint, and the reality that there isn't a right or wrong solution. Your access to knowledge on virtually any item, product, or service is limitless in the digital age. It's no longer possible for companies to hide behind false commercials, pitches, or trademarks.

Significant noncompliance failures are not usually the consequence of deliberate wrongdoing. Defects in corporate governance and risk management are sometimes to blame. Given the rapid rate of change and innovation in your sector, it's crucial to remember that you're here to leave an indelible mark. Your standards provide practical assistance for typical compliance issues, ensuring that your employees always have access to the most up-to-date ethical information. The layers of compliance processes are expanding at organisations all around the world. At first glance, this appears to make sense: increasing the number of laws aimed at prohibiting unethical or harmful activity appears to be the most apparent and easy way of doing so.

However, a checkbox mindset that creates the perception of risk reduction without actually doing so is one of the most disconcerting and unexpected outcomes of a sole concentration on ethics-as-compliance.

Furthermore, unless taken carefully, a compliance-focused strategy to prevent unethical activity can stiflean organisation's ability to innovate and take calculated risks.

How can you be certain that you will be able to avoid the danger of noncompliance?

To begin, let us define statutory compliance and the numerous compliances necessary for Indian payroll.

The term "statutory" refers to rules and regulations that are "of or linked to legislation." Adherence is synonymous with compliance. Thus, statutory compliance entails following laws and regulations. Statutory compliance in human resources refers to the legal framework that an organisation must follow while interacting with its employees.

Every country has its own set of state and central labour rules that businesses must follow. Dealing with statutory compliance necessitates that businesses be current on all labour legislation in their jurisdiction. Organisations are also required to follow them. Noncompliance with these requirements may land a business in a lot of legal trouble, including penalties and fines. As a result, every firm invests a significant amount of money, effort, and time to fulfil compliance obligations ranging from professional tax to minimum wage legislation. To assist with this, the corporation seeks professional guidance from labour and tax law specialists.

To deal with a difficult regulatory environment, every organisation should be well-versed in labour laws and pay attention to all rules. They must devise effective methods for maintaining compliance while minimising risks. The complexity of running a business has skyrocketed, making it extremely difficult to stay on top of every organisational's operational aspects. As previously noted, organisations seek the assistance of statutory compliance specialists whose primary goal is to ensure compliance with the ever-changing regulatory environment.

Furthermore, many organisations offer statutory compliance management services as well as a deeper grasp of the regulatory environment and specialised services to enterprises. They simplify the procedure from start to finish. They expedite the procedure from the daily maintenance of mandated forms and registers through filing and reporting.

We've all heard of corporations that pushed the boundaries of compliance, looking for loopholes in regulations, only to be discovered breaking the rules. The end result? To mention a few, large penalties and severe reputational harm leaving aside the worst-case circumstances, noncompliance is never fun. However, ensuring that your organisation's activities are entirely compliant with the law may be a time-consuming and difficult procedure.

In an increasingly complicated, multi-stakeholder environment, how can you be an ethical corporate citizen? This is the most critical question confronting today's enterprises, large and small, local and global. I would like to share few key measures that any organisation must follow to achieve compliance.

- Your organisation is not compliant by default. It is a continual process of scanning for new laws and regulations, identifying how they affect your company, modifying policies, executing policy changes, and monitoring.
- Keep track of which rules and regulations relate to your company and remain up-to-date on any changes. When you are prepared for forthcoming changes, you are less

likely to feel overwhelmed when new laws are implemented.

- Software systems with a "identify new rules" capability make this procedure easier by automatically recognising important legislative changes using Natural Language Processing.
- Small and developing businesses, in particular, may unknowingly violate the law. To avoid this, ensure that the organisation's activities are transparent. Furthermore, hiring professionals or involving consultants is recommended to ensure that everything is in order. This enables owners and workers to seek guidance when necessary in order to verify that activities and processes are compliant.
- Use specialist insights to design a software solution that exactly meets the demands of your organisation to ensure compliance.
- Changes in policy, in particular, may not always be easily absorbed by the workforce, and workers may be hesitant to modify procedures in their daily workflows. It is critical to include HR in this process.
- Most crucially, ensure that corporate policies and processes are effectively communicated. Part of this is ensuring that they are adequately recorded and easily accessible, both digitally and physically. Additionally, ensure that employees understand why policies and procedures are the way they are or have changed.
- Replace monotonous duties with automation whenever feasible to ensure your knowledge employees follow corporate policy.
- You may want to consider constructing a reward system for employees that comply as well as developing consequences in the event of infractions.

- Internal audits are an excellent tool for identifying weak and poor practises that contribute to noncompliance. Internal audits may concentrate on the organisation's financial, operational, technical, or regulatory elements. When examining compliance, it is critical that an internal auditor be unbiased and follow commonly accepted auditing standards (GAAS). Furthermore, strong compliance software frequently includes capabilities for organising documents as well as the ability to automatically produce audit trails to readily show compliance.
- Be Informed is a low-code development platform that assists enterprises all around the world in developing solutions to assure compliance.

While a few organisations have been created to enable humanity to thrive and grow, most businesses have traditionally been built on flawed principles that focus on efficiency through control. This often comes to the fore when we see organisations attempting to institute change using methodologies that intend to remove humanity from the process. Companies are groups of people who work for other groups of people. We set ourselves up for failure by removing the "human element."

It has been noted many times, but it bears repeating: the pandemic's massive magnitude and velocity of work-related change could never have been predicted prior to COVID-19. Employees began working from home, and families began homeschooling their children for months at a time. In a couple of months, millions of doses of very potent vaccinations were manufactured and distributed. However, they were motivated by a need to prioritise human needs, to keep everyone safe, to maintain salaries, and to demonstrate compassion for one another. Despite all of the negative consequences and disruption, there is a genuine desire to harness the force of change and utilise it for long-term benefit—not just for organisations to succeed but also to contribute to the overall health of human society and the world. It all starts with purpose, and a human-centered corporation prioritises humans.

The importance of organisational purpose has been hotly debated, with many organisations attempting to promote the concept of doing "meaningful work" as a method of winning market share. Authenticity is essential, so ifan organisation truly wants to make the world a better place, developing meaning and purpose with a human centre shouldn't be too difficult.

However, if the intention is only to give lip service in order to promote sales, defining those legitimate credentials may be more difficult. Once an organisation has defined its ultimate goal, it must convey it simply and effectively to all stakeholders, including consumers, workers, and others.

Trust is vital for fostering respect between employees and employers, and human-centered organisations foster this by recognising the worth and symbiotic nature of both the customer and the employee and treating both with equal regard. Once we acknowledge that all of our interactions, from employee to customer, are interrelated, companies can apply the same paradigm to their relationship with the larger societal framework, looking at the connection to the natural environment and how the organisation is fostering that relationship. This is not a typical corporate strategy, but we live in a complicated and more risky context where global warming, biodiversity loss, and the impact of mass inequality threaten to adversely influence everyone.

As a result, organisations must play an important role in pushing change, but fresh views and a shift in how these challenges are addressed are required for them to become the new norm. Historically, most organisations have recognised and adhered to the concept of being a learning organisation, devoting time and resources to learning. The difficulty, however, is that most approaches have historically relied on concepts that support what we believe we already know about our organisations and the world around us.

"We must do things differently to break this cycle and discover fresh answers to the complicated difficulties that today's businesses confront."

Human-centered organisations are the new breed of learning organisations. Recognising that organisations are basically people working in the service of others, they will only thrive if their people grow. However, we can only progress by learning something new, and in reality, this requires actively challenging attitudes and behaviours, identities, phobias, and prior experiences. Human-centered organisations strive for one of two outcomes: performing different work or doing work differently. With the advent of machine learning and automation in recent years, this has become increasingly relevant. While certain positions still have standard methods, the majority of functions are becoming far more fluid. Job descriptions, employees requirements, and competency listings are all set to become obsolete.

As a result, human-centered organisations recognise, foster, and promote people's learning so that they may pivot and shift in an agile manner, keeping pace with and seeing ahead of the market and wider social environment as needed. They also recognise the significance of democratising the learning process and investing in learning and development at all levels, not just those in positions of senior leadership. Furthermore, this learning agenda goes beyond the workplace to create agility by maximising everyone's potential through whole-person development.

This is not a simple process, and the deeper or more disruptive the new learning, the more difficult we find it because big change inevitably disrupts the status quo. On a personal level, it might be difficult to accept current preconceptions and our own participation within those beliefs. Traditional hierarchies, which this form of learning seeks to dismantle, have long been founded on the core concept that people's responsibilities are based on unassailable specialised knowledge and experience. Accepting the idea that we are continuously learning, however, flips this premise on its head. Importantly, genuine change occurs when this learning is used in practise, or "in the flow of work."

Learning cannot occur in the framework of a human-centered organisation without "direct interaction." Experiential learning, in particular, must be social, relational, and contextual. To fully thrash out the nuts and bolts and stress test them to ensure they are fit for purpose, it takes people working through their development together, ripping ideas apart and pushing them. This should apply at all hierarchical levels, from line managers and leaders to those with no direct reports. Everyone's contribution and influence should be acknowledged and realised, since only through this degree of challenge can human-centered learning and transformation occur at the pace and scale required to allow significant change inside organisations and beyond.

At its most basic level, cultural transformation is all about ensuring that you're only promoting behaviour that is completely consistent with your beliefs and goals. It's a seemingly easy notion, but, in practice, it may be exceedingly difficult to execute. Get some help if you don't know how to accomplish something or if you're not sure whether you're doing it correctly. Outside eyes and ears are typically better at recognising where you could be promoting exactly the sort of behaviour you claim you want to stop, even if unwittingly.

Business ethics is a prominent subject in the media, society at large, and academics these days. Even corporations are adding ethical discussion into their internal discourse and governance procedures.

- How is it put into reality and how can it be reconciled with market competitiveness?
- Does it include people as aware beings with a sense of morality?

For examples of scandals and questionable behaviour, look at Enron, Lehman Brothers, Volkswagen, Siemens, and France Télécom, as well as Bernie Madoff's Ponzi scheme. On the other hand, there are excellent instances of corporate ethics at work, such as François Michelin's people-centered vision, Bill George's leadership at Medtronic, and AES Corporation's basic values, which are still in use today. How you handle the ambiguities, the grey regions of ethics, which, as you've stated, aren't black and white, will decide your leadership effectiveness?

How can you get the best outcome out of one bad scenario versus another bad situation?

Because of the ethics scandals that have stopped companies and individuals from achieving their goals, businesses and the accounting profession have never been under such close ethical scrutiny. Understanding why ethical behaviour is so vital to achievement, as well as being aware of possible hazards, is critical to your own success. The notion that business is just about making money no longer holds water in the twenty-first century, as businesses all over the world are eschewing conventional distinctions in order to prosper. Remember that in order to survive and develop in this competitive market, businesses must have solid corporate governance and adhere to all company regulations.

According to a shocking report released at the end of 2019, nearly one hundred Fortune 500 companies skipped paying federal taxes the previous year, including well-known names such as Amazon, Chevron, and Starbucks. According to data conducted by the anti-poverty organisation Action Aid International, the article was published in The Gurdian, huge internet giants like Facebook, Google, and Microsoft have all failed to pay taxes in poor nations where governments struggle to satisfy basic healthcare and educational needs.

Digital marketers now have a plethora of tools at their disposal to acquire massive amounts of data from their customers and develop richer, more personalised marketing methods. Consumers have rightfully grown more anxious about what happens to their personal data when they offer it to the organisations with whom they do business in an age where notions such as surveillance capitalism and targeted advertising dominate practically every part of the Internet.

More individuals than ever before are concerned about their societal effect in today's environment. In the age of COVID-19, it's safe to say that ethical marketing has taken on a whole new meaning. In the course of a year, brands have been compelled to make fast adjustments to their marketing tactics and how they pivot their services towards their customers. While it may appear that the crisis has brought effective marketing initiatives to a halt, other research suggests otherwise.

It's easy to ignore a new technology's potential drawbacks when it arrives with significant advantages. Technology has come to control much of our modern work and personal lives. While technological advancements have allowed us to work from home, acquire a wide range of goods, occupy ourselves, and even receive remote medical treatment, they have also raised severe concerns. Concerns about anything from privacy to human behaviour to the environment are paired with the evident advantages of broad technology use. While executives are among the most enthusiastic supporters of technology solutions to problems, they are also acutely aware of the ethical issues that come with them.

"It takes 20 years to build a reputation and five minutes to ruin it. If you think about that, you'll do things differently." -Warren Buffet

An organisational Ombudsman is a neutral or impartial dispute resolution practitioner whose primary responsibility is to provide independent, impartial, confidential, and informal assistance to managers and employees, clients, and/or other stakeholders of a corporation, university, or non-governmental organisation. Ombudsman (om budz man) is a Swedish term that literally means "representative." At its most basic level, an

Ombudsman is a person who aids individuals and groups in resolving disagreements or problems. This post is known by a variety of titles and names, including "Ombudsman," "ombudsperson," and "ombuds."

The classical Ombudsman first arose in Sweden in the early nineteenth century as an independent high-level public official who was appointed by constitutional or legislative provisions to supervise government administrative actions and was answerable to the parliament or legislature. This approach has been imitated and altered in a variety of ways in a variety of nations and environments. Organisational Ombudsmen, classical Ombudsmen, and advocate Ombudsmen are all various sorts of ombudsmen with varied functions, functional tasks, and norms of practice.

The main responsibilities of an organisational "Ombudsman" are to work with individuals and groups within an organisation to explore and assist them in determining options for resolving conflicts, problematic issues, or concerns, as well as to bring systemic concerns to the organisation's attention for resolution. Some organisational ombuds are hired from inside an organisation, accepting this post after demonstrating the above-mentioned qualities and establishing a well-known reputation for integrity, confidentiality, and awareness of organisational procedures across functions in prior roles. When recruiting from the outside, an organisation would frequently look for someone with a background in dispute resolution and/or who has earned a reputation as an "Ombudsman" via past organisational experience. Ombudsmen who come from outside the organisation, with no prior experience or connections, may be able to offer new viewpoints, and the perception of neutrality may be reinforced. Organisations may also employ the services of an independent Ombudsman.

An organisational Ombudsman is a designated neutral or impartial dispute resolution practitioner whose primary responsibility is to provide independent, impartial, confidential, and informal assistance to managers and employees, clients, and/or other stakeholders of a corporation, university, non-governmental organisation, government agency, or other entity. The organisational Ombudsman should ideally have no other job or responsibilities as an independent and unbiased employee. This is to ensure independence and neutrality, as well as to avoid actual or apparent conflicts of interest.

An organisational Ombudsman gives opportunities for people with problems, including whistleblowers, who want to bring their complaints forward securely and effectively, using an alternative dispute resolution (ADR) mindset. Additionally, an organisational Ombudsman gives counselling on ethics and other management concerns, facilitates dispute resolution through mediation, and assists in the development of policies. Additionally, an organisational Ombudsman gives coaching on ethics and other management concerns, provides mediation to aid dispute resolution, assists people who feel harassed or discriminated against, and helps permit safe upward feedback. The organisational Ombudsman, in general, aids employees and managers in navigating bureaucracy and dealing with complaints and issues.

"Play fair, be prepared for others to play dirty, and don't let them drag you into the mud."- Richard Branson

Employers who were unaware of the traditional Ombudsman function but recognised the advantage of a senior manager who is a neutral, impartial, confidential, and informal problem-solver and systems change agent have frequently re-invented the role of organisational Ombudsman. Examples first arose in the United States in the 1920s, and they are likely to have appeared in a variety of civilizations. In many businesses, the organisational Ombudsman is viewed as a component of or a link to a complaint system, but the office is designed to operate independently of all normal line and employees management and to report to the CEO or Board of Directors.

What are the important duties of an organisational ombudsman?

- Listens and comprehends difficulties while keeping an objective when it comes to facts. The ombudsman does not listen in order to pass judgement or to determine who is correct or incorrect. The ombudsman listens to comprehend the problem from the individual's point of view. This is a crucial phase in the process of creating resolution possibilities.
- An ombudsman assists in rephrasing difficulties and formulating and evaluating choices for individuals. This assists people in identifying the various parties' interests in the issues and focusing efforts on potential solutions to suit those interests. Individuals are guided or coached on how to interact directly with other parties, including how to use the organisation's formal resolution options. An ombudsman frequently strives to assist people in improving their ability and confidence in directly expressing their problems.
- Individuals are sent to relevant services for conflict resolution. An ombudsman may connect people to one or more official organisational resources that may be

able to help them resolve their problems.

- An ombudsman assists in bringing concerns to the attention of official resolution mechanisms. When a person is unable or reluctant to express a complaint directly, the ombudsman can assist by giving the concern a voice and/or raising awareness of the issue among competent decision-makers within the organisation.
- An ombudsman facilitates informal conflict settlement. An ombudsman can assist parties in resolving disputes through various forms of informal mediation.
- An ombudsman identifies new concerns and possibilities for the organisation's structural change. The ombuds' unique position allows them to share unedited information that can lead to better understanding and resolution of situations. The ombudsman is a source of new issue discovery and early warning, as well as systemic reform ideas to enhance existing systems.

Would you like to know more about ombudsman' skills-roles-responsibilities?

- Active listening, effective communication with a diverse range of people, remaining nonjudgmental, having the courage to speak up and address problems at higher levels within an organisation, problem-solving and analytical ability, and conflict resolution skills are among the most important skills of an effective ombudsperson. The acquisition and demonstration of the skill set indicated above is more significant than a specific professional history or academic degree.

- Outstanding ombudspeople from a variety of professional and academic backgrounds, including scientists, human resource experts, mediators, academics, line managers, engineers, attorneys, accountants, and consultants.
- The ombudsman hears and comprehends concerns while staying objective in his or her assessment of the facts.
- The ombudsman does not listen in order to pass judgement or to determine who is correct or incorrect.
- The ombudsman listens to comprehend the problem from the individual's point of view. This is a crucial phase in the process of creating resolution possibilities.
- The Ombudsman provides support in reframing situations and establishing and evaluating choices for individuals. This aids people in identifying the interests of various parties involved in the issues and concentrating efforts on them.
- There is no cost, it is independent of the government, and it is non-partisan. Reports on systematic concerns occurring within an agency or with the performance of a government program may be released. Bad practises may be addressed.
- The state ombudsman can offer both mediation and investigation. It is impossible to provide a quick response to complicated situations. The complainant has no control over the investigation; the ombudsman does not explicitly act for the complainant, and they have the authority to refuse to handle a specific case.
- Citizens' complaints of abuse of discretionary power, maladministration, or administrative inefficiency are investigated by the ombudsman, who then takes necessary action. They are given extensive authority for

this reason. The complainant is not required to present any proof before the ombudsman in order to establish his case.

- The ombudsman's job and responsibility is to determine whether or not the complaint was legitimate. He's even capable of acting on his own.
- An ombudsman can provide a remedy to the aggrieved party since, unlike a regular court, his powers are unrestricted. In most cases, the ombudsman is a judge, a lawyer, or a high-ranking official with impeccable morals, ethics, and probity. Because the ombudsman is appointed by Parliament, he is not hired by any administrative body or the Executive.
- An ombudsman is unaffected by political affiliations and is able to think and act rationally. Even Parliament has no say in how he carries out his responsibilities. He submits a report to Parliament detailing citizen reactions to the government. He also offers his own suggestions for removing the sources of complaints. Those reports receive a lot of attention. All of his reports appear in national newspapers as well. In a nutshell, he is the "watchdog" or "public safety valve" against mal-administration.

Ombudsmen exist for a single purpose: to assist individuals and organisations. They help employees by providing them with someone or a team with whom they can have confidential discussions about bribery, their boss's drug use, sexual harassment, personal conflicts, and other issues. Some employees view HR, compliance officials, and supervisors as business agents whose role it is to safeguard the firm's interests rather than the employees'. They don't know how an investigation will end, and they're frightened the law won't protect them, just like those who are hesitant to report something to the police. This assists people in identifying the various parties' interests in the issues and focusing efforts on potential solutions to suit those interests.

The ombudsman assists or trains people in dealing directly with other parties, including the use of the organisation's official resolution options. An ombudsman frequently strives to assist people in improving their ability and confidence in directly expressing their problems. Individuals are referred to suitable resolution resources by the ombudsman. An ombudsman may connect people to one or more official organisational resources that might be able to help them resolve their problems. When conducting investigations, the ombudsman always takes an objective and unbiased approach while also adhering to procedural fairness. In the course of an inquiry, the ombudsman obtains confidential information.

Some organisational ombudsmen are hired from inside an organisation, accepting this post after demonstrating the above-mentioned qualities and establishing a well-known reputation for honesty, confidentiality, and understanding of organisational procedures across functions in prior roles. When recruiting from the outside, an organisation would frequently look for someone with a history of dispute resolution and/or who has earned a reputation as an ombudsman via previous organisational experience. Ombudsmen who come from outside the organisation, with no prior experience or connections, may be able to offer new viewpoints, and the perception of neutrality may be improved. Organisations may also use the services of an independent ombudsman who is hired on a contract basis.

Making realistic advice concerning serious issues is a priority for the ombudsman. The ombudsman will only offer recommendations if he or she believes they would benefit the public. The ombudsman also evaluates the financial implications of the recommendations for agencies. Ombudsmen provide their services for free, making them available to anyone who cannot afford to pursue their grievances via the courts. They are dedicated to seeking individual remedies as well as systemic reforms in the work of the organisations under their supervision, both individually and collectively, if they find systemic inadequacies. They can usually conduct a single inquiry into many complaints about the same subject, minimising redundancy and unnecessary expense.

Corruption is a societal blight that obstructs healthy, balanced social and economic development. The lack of adequate protection for complainants reporting corruption, willful misuse of power, or willful misuse of discretion that causes demonstrable loss to the government or the commission of a criminal offence by a public servant is one of the impediments to eliminating corruption in the government and public sector undertakings. It was determined to pass a separate law to offer proper protection to those who expose corruption or wilful misuse of authority or discretion that causes the government to lose money, or who reveal the conduct of a criminal offence by a public official.

Raising the alarm about problematic practises early enough can help guarantee that issues are discovered before it's too late, preventing tragedies ranging from widespread consumer maltreatment to death. Whistleblowing processes should encourage individuals to report problems through proper channels before they become a severe problem, resulting in unfavourable publicity, regulatory scrutiny, penalties, and/or compensation for the organisation. The Whistle Blowers Protection Act, 2011, is an Act passed by the Indian Parliament in 2011 that establishes a mechanism to investigate allegations of public servant corruption and abuse of power, as well as to protect anyone who reports alleged wrongdoing in government bodies, projects, and offices.

- What is the definition of a "*whistleblower*"?
- Why do whistleblowers face all kinds of retaliation in the pursuit of the truth?
- What does the whistleblower's abuse cycle look like most of the time?
- How do you blow the whistle without jeopardising your job?
- What may be included in non-disclosure agreement settlements?
- What do whistleblowers have to say about it?
- What can be done to ensure that whistleblowers are protected?

A whistleblower is someone who reveals confidential knowledge or actions that are unlawful, unethical, or incorrect within a business or public institution. The name is claimed to have been invented by Ralph Nader, a prominent American civic activist, in the early 1970s to avoid the negative connotations of words like "informer" and "snitch."

A whistleblower is someone who reports or exposes unlawful, immoral, or unethical action or activity by a person, public company, or private firm. Alternatively, it generates a suspicion of misconduct. Many businesses have their own whistleblower policy, which outlines the kinds of actions that are covered as well as the steps to take if an employee wants to make a protected disclosure. This policy is intended to help and encourage workers to hold the organisation and its employees accountable while also promoting strong ethical and moral standards.

Whistleblowing occurs when an employee, contractor, or supplier moves outside of the standard management channels to disclose suspected workplace malfeasance, i.e., speaking up in a private way. This can be done through the organisation's internal channels (internal whistleblowing) or to an external entity such as a regulator (external whistleblowing). While public disclosure to the media can be seen as whistleblowing, the focus of this study is on formally mandated routes. A worker can report things that aren't right, are unlawful, or if someone at work isn't performing their job, such as:

- Someone's health and safety is at risk
- Environmental damage
- A criminal offence
- The firm isn't following the law
- Covering up wrongdoing

When a whistleblower informs higher-ranking employees of wrongdoing inan organisation, disloyalty, inappropriate conduct, indiscipline, insubordination, and disobedience are common topics for internal whistleblowing.

External whistleblowing occurs when wrongdoings are disclosed to those outside the institution, such as the media, public interest organisations, or law enforcement authorities. Alumni whistleblowing occurs when a former employee ofan organisation acts as a source of information.

Open whistleblowing occurs when the identity of the whistleblowers is disclosed. Personal whistle blowing occurs when an organisation's wrongdoings solely affect one person, and revealing such wrongdoings is referred to as personal whistle blowing.

When information about wrongdoings or unethical behaviour by government employees becomes public,whenan organisation discloses wrongdoing, it is referred to as corporate whistleblowing.

Impersonal whistle blowing occurs when the wrongdoing is intended to damage others.

Various whistle-blowers have been threatened, harassed, and even murdered on several occasions. Satyendra Dubey, an engineer, was assassinated in November 2003 after blowing the whistle on a corruption case involving the Golden Quadrilateral project of the National Highways Authority of India. Two years later, Shanmughan Manjunath, an Indian Oil Corporation officer, was killed for shutting down a petrol pump that was selling contaminated fuel. The Whistle Blowers Protection Act, 2011, is an Act of the Indian Parliament that establishes a mechanism for investigating allegations of public servant corruption and abuse of power, as well as provides protection to anyone who exposes alleged wrongdoing in government bodies, projects, and offices. It's possible that the misconduct takes the form of fraud, corruption, or mismanagement. Fraud, corruption, or mismanagement are examples of misconduct. The Act was endorsed by the Indian Cabinet as part of a campaign to clean up the country's bureaucracy, and it was enacted by the Lok Sabha on December 27, 2011. When the Rajya Sabha approved the Bill on February 21, 2014, and the President gave his assent on May 9, 2014, it became an Act.

Comparison of the 2015 Bill with the 2013 Amendments to the Whistle-blowers Protection Act of 2014. On February 21, 2014, Parliament enacted the Whistle-blowers Protection Act of 2014. On August 5, 2013, after the Bill was approved by the Lok Sabha, various modifications were circulated in the Rajya Sabha. However, when the Bill was enacted by the Rajya Sabha in 2014, these revisions were not included. On May 11, 2015, the Whistle-blowers Protection (Amendment) Bill, 2015 was tabled in the Lok Sabha. According to the Statement of Objects and Reasons, this Bill was submitted to give effect to prior revisions that were not passed. The provisions of the 2015 Bill are compared to those of the 2013 amendments in the table below. Despite opposition from the Opposition, the Lok Sabha (India's bicameral Parliament's lower chamber) enacted a Bill to alter the Whistleblowers Protection Act 2011 (passed by Parliament in 2014) on May 13, 2015. The Bill will now be presented to the Rajya Sabha for consideration (the upper house). It has been suggested that the Bill is being used to diminish the Act's effect.

A public interest disclosure may be made before a competent authority by anyone, including a public official or an NGO, according to the Act. Regardless of the prohibitions of the Official Secrets Act of 1923, this would apply. Certain items were excluded from disclosure under Section 8 of the Act, including information likely to jeopardise India's sovereignty and integrity, the state's security, cordial relations with other nations, public order, decency, or morality, or information relating to contempt of court, defamation, or incitement to an offence. As may be the case with the revelation of the Cabinet of the Union Government or any of its committees‘ actions, as would be the case with the publication of the State Government's Cabinet or any of its committees' sessions. Other grounds for exempting material from disclosure are included in the amendment bill, including: Unless such information has been revealed to the complaint under the terms of the Right to Information Act, 2005, it relates to commercial confidence, trade secrets, or intellectual property, the revelation of which would undermine a third party's competitive position. Unless such information has been revealed to the complaint under the requirements of the Right to Information Act, 2005, information that is available to a person in his fiduciary function or connection; information that might jeopardise a person's life or physical safety, or reveal the source of confidential information or assistance provided for law enforcement or security objectives; information that might obstruct the investigation, arrest, or prosecution of criminals.

A competent body must recommend a banned disclosure to a government authority for final approval. The Bill, on the other hand, does not establish the requisite credentials or the process for appointing this authority. Other nations‘ whistle-blower laws similarly limit the sharing of certain types of information. These include national security and intelligence material obtained in a fiduciary role, as well as any disclosure expressly forbidden by law. It is critical for every firm to have clear communication throughout the organisation and to set appropriate limits. Employees require a secure and private channel to express their concerns in the event of a problem. In this scenario, whistleblowing software is critical in providing employees with the opportunity to report wrongdoing.

You will come upon these ethical concerns in your business at some point. Even if you take all the essential safeguards, you should always be ready to deal with them. Use them as a learning experience in order to establish a stronger and more ethical business in this market. Organisations can learn from their errors, and the best way to do so is to communicate any issues to top management. If you have suspicions of criminal behaviour, have seen wrongdoing, or have ethical issues, you can express them anonymously by calling an anonymous whistleblowing hotline. While it is critical to speak out when you see unethical activity, the greater the dangers to the company or your direct management, the more pressure you may feel to go along with or overlook the behaviour, especially if blowing the whistle might jeopardise your career.

Consider that, according to the 2016 National Business Ethics study conducted by the Ethics and Compliance Initiative and published by The New York Times, 53% of employees who reported ethical violations in their workplaces suffered some type of retribution. Using euphemisms to soften the gravity of unethical behaviour, delaying confronting the behaviour, or reasoning that most people would go along with the breach anyhow are all behaviours that may fester, driving off excellent employees, damaging careers, and putting the company in jeopardy.

Recent high-profile ethical issues, particularly those involving discrimination and sexual harassment, have shed focus on unethical workplace behaviour and how such failings may infect employee relationships, business policies, and operations. According to the Ethics & Compliance Initiative's 2018 Global Benchmark on Workplace Ethics, 30% of employees in the United States directly saw wrongdoing in the previous 12 months, a figure close to the global average for misbehaviour observation. These ethical infractions typically go undetected or unaddressed, and when they are coupled, they may cost a lot of money. Unethical business activities have caused more than half of the greatest bankruptcies in the last 30 years, including Enron, Lehman Brothers, and WorldCom, and can have a greater economic impact, estimated at $1.228 trillion in accordance with the Society for Human Resource Management.

Each is a significant example of corporate corruption, and the list is far from exhaustive. The list excludes undetected corruption, as well as scandals in government, education, healthcare, the military, money laundering, and tax evasion. It's worth reflecting on how difficult it is to maintain secrets these days. We live in a time when communication is instantaneous and inexpensive. Everyone has a camera-equipped cellphone. A flash drive may hold the equivalent of a file cabinet's worth of records. Corporate criminality would vanish without a strong mechanism to force employees to remain silent in the face of public scrutiny. Thousands of employees must be participating in corporate corruption. How can corruption continue when there are so many witnesses? Whistleblower retribution and blacklisting are the obvious solutions. Whistleblowers don't speak up because they are afraid of losing their jobs. Understanding the motives of employees is the first step in reducing corruption.

How to safeguard Whistleblowers'?

Why are average employees so deafeningly quiet? What is the mechanism that keeps people silent? Once you understand this, you may alter employee incentives such that similarly situated employees make different decisions in the future. You must also educate the public about the issue. There are several misunderstandings. The majority of individuals believe that corporate fraud and criminality are uncommon. They believe their boss does not and would not breach the law under any circumstances.

Whistleblowers are viewed as troublemakers, or worse, and they believe corporate wrongdoing is unimportant. These findings are not supported by the facts. Yes, there are whistleblower protection laws and anti-retaliation procedures in place, but the public is well aware that whistleblowers are frequently punished and subjected to retaliation. Yes, there are whistleblower protection laws and anti-retaliation rules in place, but nonetheless, most people are aware that whistleblowers are frequently punished and retaliated against.

As a result, they require a discreet, informal, unbiased, and independent resource to assist them in dealing with such difficulties. An ombudsman can help with that. Yes, there are whistleblower protection laws and anti-retaliation rules in place, but nonetheless, most people are aware that whistleblowers are frequently punished and retaliated against. As a result, they require a discreet, informal, unbiased, and independent resource to assist them in dealing with such difficulties. An ombudsman can help with that.

Thousands of German car industry employees knew their employers were breaking the law in the years leading up to the VW diesel-gate incident, yet they all remained silent. Several of the world's major corporations were involved in a worldwide criminal conspiracy. Eleven million automobiles were sold worldwide with defeat devices, produced, and fitted. Over a five-year period, these vehicles accounted for 40% of VW's sales. It was a massive ruse. Because of the trickery, massive amounts of NOx, the substance that produces acid rain, were released into the environment. VW was fined $25 billion, Mercedes was fined 870 million euros, Porsche was fined $600 million, and BMW was fined $11 million. The system was clearly illegal, and a considerable number of employees were aware of it for more than five years.

Dieselgate and similar situations should serve as a wake-up call. We must understand that corruption, even by the world's most prestigious corporations, is a daily occurrence. It's past time to put a stop to this corruption, and there's a simple method to do so: promote whistleblowers. A hundred thousand fatalities may have been spared if Chinese officials had listened to coronavirus whistleblower Dr. Li Wenliang. The illicit emissions would have been stopped years sooner if any of the VW employees had gone to the press. Understanding why informed insiders remain silent about corruption, changing the rules of the game so insiders speak out, and ensuring regulators listen to and react correctly are the most effective paths to eliminating corporate wrongdoing.

Corporate corruption is on the rise across the world. Audi, Barclays, Boeing, BMW, BP, CBS, Deloitte, Equifax, E&Y, FaceTime, Facebook, FoxxConn, FIFA, Fyre, J&J, Kobe Steel, KPMG, Nissan, Purdue, PWC, Rolls Royce, Samsung, Theranos, Turing Pharma, Mossack Fonseca, Uber, VW, Walmart, Wells, WeWork, Wirecard, and 1MBD are among the companies that Adelphia, AIG, Anderson, Banniter, Barclays, Bear, Deutsche, Enron, Global Crossing, Healthsouth, HIH, Lehman, Madoff, Northrup, Olympus, Parmalat, Siemens, SocGen, Tyco, Waste Mgmt, UBS, and Worldcom join the classics: Adelphia, AIG, Anderson, Banniter, Barclays, Bear, Deutsche, Enron, Global Crossing,

Wells, WeWork, Wirecard, and 1MBD are just some of them. As you read the list, your vision blurs.

What ethical principles executives must imbibe?

- Ethical principles are ethical beliefs put into active language that provide norms or regulations specifying the types of conduct that an ethical person should or should not engage in. The features and ideals that most people connect with ethical behaviour are included in the following list of principles.
- Honesty In all of their transactions, ethical executives are honest and truthful, and they do not intentionally mislead or deceive people by misrepresentations, overstatements, partial truths, selective omissions, or any other method.
- Integrity ethical executives demonstrate personal integrity and courage of conviction by doing what they believe is right, even when it is difficult; they are principled, honorable, and upright, and they will fight for their beliefs.
- Trustworthiness Executives who act ethically are deserving of our trust. They are open and honest in providing pertinent information and correcting factual errors, and they make every reasonable effort to keep their pledges and obligations in letter and spirit. They do not use overly technical or legalistic interpretations of agreements in order to justify non-compliance or construct arguments for avoiding their obligations.
- Loyalty & ethical CEOs are trustworthy, demonstrating integrity and dedication to people and organisations via friendship in difficult times, support, and devotion to duty; they do not use or divulge confidential information for personal gain. They protect their

capacity to make unbiased professional judgements by avoiding undue influence and conflicts of interest as much as possible. They are loyal to their employers and coworkers, and if they leave, they give appropriate notice, respect their former employer's private information, and refuse to engage in any actions that take unfair advantage of their prior positions.

- Fairness in all transactions, ethical executives are fair and just. Fair people are committed to fairness, equitable treatment for all people, tolerance for and acceptance of variety, and they are open-minded; they are prepared to recognise when they are mistaken and, if necessary, adjust their stances and ideas.
- Ethical CEOs are loving, empathetic, benevolent, and kind, and they strive to achieve their corporate goals with the least amount of harm and the greatest amount of positive benefit.
- Ethical CEOs respect the human dignity, autonomy, privacy, rights, and interests of all those affected by their actions; they are courteous and treat everyone with equal respect and decency, regardless of gender, ethnicity, or country of origin. Observe the law.
- Ethical leaders follow the laws, rules, and regulations that govern their businesses. Excellence is a passion for me. Ethical executives strive for excellence in their work, are well-informed and prepared, and are always looking to improve their skills in all areas of responsibility.
- Ethical executives are aware of the responsibilities and opportunities that come with their position of leadership, and they strive to be positive ethical role models through their own actions and by assisting in the creation of an environment that values principled

reasoning and ethical decision-making.

- Ethical executives strive to safeguard and enhance the company's good name and employee morale by engaging in no activity that may be seen as disrespectful to others and by taking whatever steps are necessary to address or avoid improper behaviour on the part of others.
- Ethical Executives who are ethical recognize and take personal responsibility for the ethical character of their actions and omissions in the eyes of themselves, their colleagues, their enterprises, and their communities.

Although not all ethical infractions are as spectacular as those that grab headlines, all ethical violations are bad. When confronted with an unethical scenario or leader, consider what you value most as an individual and as a professional to help guide your reaction. Knowing whether to speak when might be a personal ethical quandary in and of itself. The "Glassdoor" effect when consumers believe internet reviews of their employers more than what organisations convey and the trust impact when employee messages become viral on social media for the sake of the organisation, companies must foster "listen-up" cultures by establishing internal reporting systems in which leadership and management listen to and encourage workers who speak out. This assures employees that their reports will be heard and taken seriously, and that things will be changed if required. Developing a culture of integrity and ethics in organisations as opposed to a an overreliance on laws and regulations. Finally, and most critically, every employee is watching for leadership accountability.

When organisations undergo fast change of CEOs and other senior executives, it can be difficult to retain a consistent identity and set of values. It is vital to choose the proper people to head the organisation. If everyone in the organisation lives the organisation's ideals, promoting from within is one strategy to guarantee those values are preserved. However, this is not always practicable or feasible. When appointing senior executives, particularly CEOs, boards must examine individuals who are not just smart, but also have the chemistry, character, and moral competence to inspire and win the hearts and minds of all stakeholders.

While continuous communication is crucial, organisations should avoid repeating the same message since it can become stale, causing employees to overlook the underlying values and principles. To stay fresh, communicating values is similar to running a marketing campaign: it must attract people's attention and employ a variety of materials, forms, and communication channels. One technique to generate this level of attention is through the power of stories. Employees throughout the business feel at ease raising legal, compliance, and ethics issues and concerns without fear of reprisal. Senior leaders hold themselves and those reporting to them accountable for adhering to the law and organisational policy, as well as shared or organisational values.

Your organisation sets a goal that looks improbable, if not unattainable (for example, a monthly sales figure or a product production number). While not intrinsically unethical. After all, having motivated leadership with ambitious corporate objectives is vital to innovation and success, the manner in which employees, and even some leaders, go about reaching the goal may raise an ethical red flag. Unrealistic goals can lead to leaders putting undue strain on their workforce, and employees may consider cutting shortcuts or breaching ethical or legal conventions to attain them. Cutting ethical corners is a shortcut that seldom pays off, and if your entire team or department is failing to reach goals, firm leadership requires that input in order to reassess those goals and re-evaluate performance.

"Whether in a developed, developing, or undeveloped country, sexual harassment in the workplace is a prevalent problem."

Atrocities against women are endemic worldwide. It is a worldwide issue that has a detrimental influence on both men and women. It occurs more frequently in the female gender. No matter how hard one tries to protect, ban, prevent, or provide remedies, violations will always occur.

As a result, women are subjected to a wide range of crimes, including female feticide, human trafficking, stalking, sexual abuse, sexual harassment, and the most horrific crime, rape. Harassment of a person (an applicant or an employee) because of their sex is illegal. Harassment can take many forms, including "sexual harassment" or unwanted sexual approaches, requests for sexual favours, and other forms of sexual verbal or physical harassment. Sexual harassment is unwanted sexual behaviour that causes a person to feel insulted, embarrassed, or intimated. Unwelcome The key word here is "behaviour." Unwelcome does not imply "forced." Even though the activity is rude and disagreeable, a victim may consent to it and actively participate in it. Whether the individual appreciated a date request, a sex-oriented remark, or both depends on all the circumstances.

Sexual harassment is defined by the Supreme Court of India as any unwelcome sexually determined behaviour (whether directly or indirectly), such as physical contact and advances; sexually coloured remarks; showing pornography.The phrase "unwelcome" is a crucial aspect of the definition. Unwelcome or unwanted conduct or acts are strictly forbidden. Sexual or romantic involvement between consenting adults at work may offend bystanders or result in a breach of company policy, but it is not sexual harassment. Actual or attempted rape or sexual assault may be included. Whistling at someone is a bad idea. Smacking lips, wailing, and kissing noises Interacting with an employee's clothing, hair, or body in any way sexually touching or rubbing against another person. It's a prevalent misconception that sexual harassment in the workplace is restricted to exchanges between male bosses and female employees.

The Sexual Harassment of Women at Workplace (Prevention, Prohibition, and Redressal) Act was passed in 2013, defining sexual harassment and outlining the procedures for filing a complaint and conducting an investigation, as well as the actions that must be taken. The Kerala High Court on Thursday, March 17, 2022 ordered organisations affiliated with the film industry to make efforts to create a joint committee to deal with allegations of sexual harassment of women under the Sexual Harassment of Women at Workplace (Prevention, Prohibition, and Redressal) Act of 2013.

Sexual harassment can occur amongst coworkers for a variety of reasons, including the following:

- Harassment of a subordinate by a superior.
- Women are capable of sexually harassing men.
- Sexual harassment of both men and women.

Offenders might be bosses, coworkers, or non-employees such as clients, vendors, and suppliers.Everything has altered as a result of the #MeToo movement. Bill Cosby, Harvey Weinstein, Charlie Rose, Kevin Spacey, Al Franken, Matt Lauer, Garrison Keillor, and other high-profile public personalities have urged institutions to take action through public forums and social media platforms. Victims of harassment have the ability to choose. They can either file an internal report and hope that their company responds appropriately, or they can choose to make their story public. In general, executives feel they understand and can define the culture of their organisation.

However, there may be a misalignment between management's concept of culture and how the rest of the business perceives it. It is a fallacy for executives to believe they always have their finger on the pulse of the organisation's culture. Organisational values are a set of explicit principles that stress the organisation's dedication to legal and regulatory compliance, honesty, and corporate ethics, among other things. Executive leadership and senior managers throughout the organisation urge workers and business partners to conduct themselves legally and ethically, as well as in line with compliance and policy requirements. In doing so, the court emphasised that film production companies must follow the law against sexual harassment, also known as the POSH Act, which was approved by Parliament in 2013. Several Indian women took part in the #MeToo campaign.

Several women in India accused influential men of sexual harassment during the #MeToo movement, including actors, stand-up comedians, and senior journalists. The Supreme Court established the Vishaka rules in a 1997 ruling. This occurred in a lawsuit brought by women's rights organisations, one of which being Vishaka.

They had launched a public interest lawsuit against Bhanwari Devi, a social worker from Rajasthan, who was allegedly gangraped. She had stopped the marriage of her one-year-old daughter in 1992, resulting in the claimed gangrape as a form of retaliation. The legally enforceable Visakha principles define sexual harassment and set three important tasks for institutions: prohibition, prevention, and reparation. The Supreme Court ordered that a Complaints Committee be established to investigate complaints of sexual harassment of women in the workplace.

In the last six years, the combination of a number of external variables has prompted businesses to treat sexual harassment in the workplace with the seriousness it deserves. Some businesses are going above and beyond the call of duty to find creative solutions to the problem of sexual harassment in the workplace. Nonetheless, numerous organisations continue to underreport the number of such instances. However, the POSH Act has compelled businesses to follow its mission and make their workplaces safer for female workers. The increasing number of female employees in the workforce, greater diversity, the transition to a less formal work environment, and pervasive technology have all contributed to the necessary transformation. Various activities are used by various organisations to monitor the pulse of their employees.

- Anonymous online surveys are conducted to find out if female employees are subjected to sexual harassment at work.
- Women-only interventions are advised to enable women to express their workplace harassment

experiences.

- Men only interventions are carried out to ensure that male coworkers are aware of the true purpose of the act and do not feel threatened or excluded.
- To guarantee that employees cohesion is at its peak, joint interventions are used.
- Several external factors have combined to provide the necessary push to treat workplace sexual harassment seriously.

The media's enormous reach is assisting in giving sexual harassment the attention it has long deserved. Because of the power of social media, a single blog post by an employee alleging workplace harassment may bring his or her organisation to its knees. In 2017, the Ministry of WCD introduced the "SHE-Box" (sexual harassment electronic box). This is an online complaint management system for female employees in the public and commercial sectors to document and resolve sexual harassment complaints. Lawyers are treating such matters seriously, and organisations such as the Sexual Harassment Law Compliance Advisory (SHLC) are helping businesses become POSH compliant by forming and training an ICC at their respective workplace.

The International Labour Organisation (ILO) established an international convention banning workplace harassment and violence on June 21, 2019. The worldwide effect of the # MeToo movement has added to the conversation about this treaty. The treaty specifically recognises that gender-based violence and harassment, including sexual harassment, can adversely impede women's access to and continuing involvement in employment.

National laws addressing workplace harassment, including sexual harassment, are required under the treaty. While there is no universal workplace violence and harassment legislation in India, the Sexual Harassment of Women at Workplace (Prevention, Prohibition, and Redressal) Act, 2013, was passed nearly six years ago with the goal of combating workplace sexual harassment.While India may be ahead in terms of legislation, the reality on the ground is quite different. According to surveys, while 38% of women have experienced or seen sexual harassment, 80% of occurrences go unreported. Sexual harassment is ubiquitous and detrimental across locations and sectors, notwithstanding the rise in reports following the # MeToo movement (due to increased awareness).

Finally, the greater goal of national and international human rights frameworks in relation to sexual harassment can only be properly realised if survivors of sexual harassment are given the opportunity to seek remedy through an unbiased and devoted commission. Governments, as well as private players, have a responsibility to work toward this realisation and ensure harassment-free workplaces for everybody.

"Organisations must recruit a diverse workforce, adopt regulations and training to encourage an equal opportunity program, and provide a welcoming environment for all types of people."

The law requires organisations to be equal-opportunity employers. Regrettably, many organisations continue to flout statutory regulations. When employees are discriminated against or harassed because of their skin colour, ethnicity, gender, disability, or age, not only an ethical but also a legal barrier is crossed. Because most businesses are concerned about the costly legal and public repercussions of discrimination and harassment, you may encounter this ethical quandary in more subtle ways, ranging from seemingly harmless off-color comments by a boss to a more persistent group think mindset that can be harmful. This might be a group perspective toward another other group (for example, ladies aren't a good match for your group). Your best response is to maintain your own beliefs while opposing such intolerant, unethical, or illegal group norms by promoting an alternate, inclusive position as the best choice for the group and the organisation. Harassment and discrimination are two of the most important ethical issues that business owners face today. If harassment or discrimination occurs in the workplace, the consequences might be disastrous for your company's finances and image.

Every business should be aware of anti-discrimination laws and regulations in place to protect employees from unfair treatment. The United States Equal Employment Opportunity Commission (EEOC) outlines numerous distinct forms of discrimination and harassment regulations that might affect your firm, including but not limited to:

- Age refers to anyone over the age of 40, as well as any ageist policy or treatment.
- Employees with physical or mental impairments are entitled to reasonable accommodation and equitable treatment.
- Equal pay is defined as equal pay for equal effort regardless of gender, ethnicity, religion, or other factors.
- Pregnant employees are given reasonable accommodations and equitable treatment.

- Employee treatment should be uniform regardless of race or ethnicity.
- Reasonable accommodations and equitable treatment are offered regardless of employee religion.
- Employee treatment should be uniform regardless of sex or gender identity.

"Ethics starts at home. A robust and well-communicated code of ethics, best articulated in terms of rules and procedures, is the cornerstone of an effective ethics and corporate compliance program."

These rules and procedures establish the organisation's culture and expected conduct for everyone who works in or with it. Being proactive also necessitates collaboration between the corporate compliance team and other departments and regulatory compliance groups in order to manage their compliance procedures, controls, templates, and schedules. This method provides the corporate compliance team with complete visibility into organisational compliance, allowing them to conduct regular or ad hoc evaluations to reduce infractions. The readiness of a business to deal with a compliance issue is crucial since it affects brand value and revenue. To that end, successful organisations must be proactive in terms of developing controls and procedures, defining accountability, and centrally maintaining compliance requirements so that they are easily available to all departments involved.

A risk-based approach to compliance and ethical management includes identifying and prioritising high-risk areas inside the company, as well as prioritising, controlling, and monitoring such risks. Compliance risks may be assessed and graded from a variety of angles, including business unit, process, and geography. Organisations can efficiently arrange control testing based on the risk rating. Issues can alternatively be sorted by grade, effect, probability, or category. There is no way for an organisation to become compliant with laws and regulations overnight. Compliance is a continual process that necessitates organisations defining new goals, leveraging technology to achieve these goals, assessing the outcomes, and then working to improve the results by setting new targets. This ongoing process will aid in the integration of corporate compliance within the business.

Every regulated organisation now needs a solid ethics and corporate compliance program. Organisations will not be able to completely comply with requirements if their employees do not adhere to corporate policies and procedures. Investing in employees training is usually a wise decision. Employees must be aware of the organisation's culture as well as its ethical limitations. Technology, in the form of learning or training management systems that make it simple to run and track different training programs, can play a key role here. Many organisations have found it beneficial to offer hotline lines where workers may anonymously report concerns about bribery, fraud, ethical breaches, discrimination, and other workplace wrongdoing. Integrating hotlines withan organisation's corporate compliance program can be beneficial since it allows for the monitoring of each issue from inception to resolution.

When there are several subsidiaries scattered across different regions, policy design must take various elements into account, such as subsidiary location and industry. The key to policy development is to ensure that policies are relevant both internationally and locally. This contributes to ensuring that there are no gaps or loopholes in compliance. Automated technologies can add value by simplifying the policy management process. Every organisation must have a compliance strategy in place to identify possible risks, develop strategies to minimise them in the short term, and create a long-term plan of action. These techniques must be extended to the departmental level, where compliance infractions and concerns may frequently jeopardise the organisation's reputation. There must be programs, procedures, and technology in place to detect, prioritise, investigate, and resolve compliance infractions and threats before they become black swan occurrences.

In order to mitigate these risks, strong regulations and practises are also required. In reality, having a strong corporate compliance program assists organisations in staying in compliance with both external standards and internal rules and practises. Training employees on policies can also help to ensure an ethical atmosphere. Building a good compliance and ethical program might be difficult at times. A corporate compliance team's major role is to design compliance strategies and programs, as well as to implement procedures and tools to detect, supervise, and mitigate compliance concerns at the enterprise level.

Furthermore, as regulatory compliance requirements increase, the corporate compliance team must engagewith specific departments and regulatory teams to supervise compliance at the departmental level. A program like this not only ensures compliance with numerous standards, but it also assists organisations in proactively identifying risks, improving ethical behaviour inside the organisation, and being audit ready.

Because of the COVID-19 epidemic, organisations have been compelled to function with a geographically distributed employees. Employees are working involuntarily from faraway areas. Many people work in lonely, unmonitored, unpleasant environments that reduce attention and motivation. The never-ending Work From Anywhere (WFA) movement may have far-reaching unintended consequences for productivity, ethics, and compliance.

While the COVID-19 epidemic hastened the trend toward working from anywhere, much more work needs to be done to address the ethics and compliance challenges that are prevalent in this new environment. While corporations and people have made significant fixed cost expenditures in transitioning from the office to remote working, the next steps need investments in technology, employees training, and organisational structure changes to reduce the risks. Employees who have no ethical reservations about defrauding the government would almost never have any difficulty submitting claims against the company.

During the COVID-19 outbreak, fraud has been extremely problematic. Because of present conditions, the possibility to get maximum benefits has arisen, and employees are opting to take advantage of it. As you can expect, this will not go unpunished, and these incidents should be reported. Taking anonymous action now will spare everyone from future troubles. The most difficult ethical challenge for any firm is to participate in any ethical battle at all. The pressures—both real and imagined—to maintain income, market footprint, and profitability almost always swamp out most decision-makers' capacity to give full priority to the practise of true ethical rigour on a daily basis.

During the epidemic, several organisations relocated to remote locations and faced new to them ethical difficulties. Surveillance of their employees is one of the most prevalent methods. While many employers offer equipment for their employees, many others do not, and instead ask them to install monitoring software. As a business partner, it is critical to ensure that the limits are properly conveyed to workers in order to avoid misunderstandings and disputes surrounding employee privacy and free expression.

Accounting software applications are even used to help people manage and keep track of their finances. As companies fight to survive in the midst of the epidemic, they tend to exaggerate their reports in order to appear successful despite the circumstances. They expose themselves to legal implications for their ability to sustain their lives. As organisations fight to survive in the midst of the epidemic, they tend to exaggerate their reports in order to appear successful despite the circumstances.

What should you do in a tumultuous world?

Organisations run by dishonest CEOs usually suffer from a toxic work culture. Leaders who take bribes, distort sales statistics and data, or press employees or business associates for favours whether personal or financial will belittle and intimidate their employees. With many companies now emphasising "cultural fit," a toxic culture may be exacerbated by repeatedly repopulating the organisation with like-minded individuals and harmful mentalities. Worse, hiring for "cultural fit" may be used as a pretext for discrimination, with extra ethical difficulties and legal ramifications.

The advancements in technology security capacity, which fall under the same umbrella as nondisclosure agreements, raise privacy issues for both clients and employees. Employers may now monitor employee activities on their laptops and other company-provided devices, and while electronic monitoring is intended to assure efficiency and production, it frequently borders on privacy invasion.

- Many employers are concerned about current and former workers stealing information, especially customer data that is exploited by groups that compete directly with the organisation. Corporate espionage occurs when intellectual property is stolen or confidential customer information is unlawfully disclosed. In order to deter these sorts of ethics infractions, companies may implement obligatory nondisclosure agreements with harsh financial penalties in the event of a violation.
- Every day, unethical behaviour and unlawful actions occur in the workplace, regardless of industry. Unethical behaviour has a negative impact on employees morale and corporate integrity. There are several instances of wrongdoing, ranging from fraud to discrimination to invasions of privacy. With the events of the COVID-19 epidemic, unethical behaviour in the workplace has also been on the increase. I have polled a group of business executives to find out what the most frequent ethical problems are in today's organisations.

Having a personal disagreement with your supervisor is one thing, but reporting someone who is acting unethically is quite another. This can be shown in apparent ways, such as tampering with figures in a report or spending corporate funds on improper activities. It can, however, appear in subtle ways, including as bullying, receiving improper gifts from suppliers, or being asked to forgo a regular process only once. Abuse of leadership power is a sad fact, with research estimating that managers are responsible for 60% of workplace wrongdoing.

I will discuss about the necessity of environmental, social, and corporate governance, as well as how the COVID-19 epidemic has accelerated the demand for racial and gender equality. Common ethical problems encountered in corporations today include decisions or lack thereof about racial and gender equality, as well as the environment.

Many businesses previously turned a blind eye to these difficulties, but this is no longer an option. Racial Equity Audit is now at the top of the priority list for many CEOs and boards of directors, as they see the impact it can have on their businesses. COVID-19 and social instability have intensified this demand since individuals have more time to focus and pay attention now that they are at home and online. Significant progress has been accomplished in recent history in terms of gender and race prejudice. New legislation and best practises have been put in place to reduce and prevent all types of prejudice. While prejudice still exists, there has been a significant improvement in recent years. Despite your progress, there are still far too many cases when incorrect judgments are made based on gender and ethnicity. Those who observe or are victims of such behaviour must be allowed to express their concerns without fear of reprisal. As a result, many organisations are turning to technology to enable employees to speak up in a secure environment and contribute to a culture of integrity.

Overpromising products or services to potential clients in order to make a contract has been a topic of discussion in the marketing business since the outbreak of the epidemic. During the marketing process, this ethical concern is a fairly prevalent inclination. Salespeople have a tendency to raise false hopes and exaggerate items or services without sharing the necessary information and method in order to complete a transaction. This ethical dilemma contradicts transparency, honesty, and the establishment of trust between the organisation and its customers. It can also cause an information gap, which leads to poor business credibility. While it may seem appealing to engage in this sort of behaviour in order to keep your business afloat, it will end up doing more harm than good for all parties involved. Integrity is essential for any business's success and ultimately decides your capacity to sustain long-term connections with your clients.

Laws and regulations have also been put in place to reduce ethical concerns about health and safety. The recent COVID-19 events have brought the significance of workplace health and cleanliness to the forefront. Increased usage of face masks, hand washing, and social isolation will likely reduce seasonal flu incidence in the future. The necessity for health and safety compliance is stronger than ever, and violations of these standards must be reported.

While this may appear to be a small issue in the wider scheme of workplace ethics, inappropriate use of the internet and business technology costs organisations a substantial amount of time, worker productivity, and corporate revenue. According to one survey, 64% of employees visit non-work-related websites during the workday. It is a waste of not just business equipment and technology, but also company time. This "little white lie" of workplace ethics may be spreading, whether you're using hourly breaks to check your social media news feed or you're aware that a coworker is using corporate technological tools to work on freelance duties. When you're working. The answer is simple: if you're working on the firm's computer on company time, don't do it, no matter how tempting it may seem. Slippery slopes are caused by ethical issues.

According to a 2019 American Management Association poll, 66% of businesses monitor internet connections, 45 percent track content, keystrokes, and keyboard time, and 43% store and examine computer files as well as employee emails. Transparency is the key to employing technology monitoring ethically. According to the same poll, 84% of respondents polled According to the same report, 84% of those organisations inform their employees that their computer behaviour is being monitored. To avoid employee monitoring becoming an ethical problem for your company, both employees and employers should be aware of the real advantages of being observed, as well as whether it is a beneficial means of establishing a record of their job performance.

There is a lot of evidence that unethical behaviour may harman organisation's reputation and cause its stock price to drop. Ethical businesses are more likely to create trust among their shareholders, workers, customers, and the general public, which is obviously beneficial to their bottom line. Remember that in order to survive and develop in this competitive market, businesses must have solid corporate governance and adhere to all company regulations. In the age of COVID-19-20, it's safe to say that ethical marketing has taken on a whole new meaning. From an ethical standpoint, and the reality that there isn't a right or wrong solution, one size doesn't fit all. Ethical brands have been forced to make fast adjustments to their marketing tactics and how they pivot their services towards their customers.

What do you believe will be the most pressing concerns in 2022 and beyond?

Aside from those already stated, it comes as no surprise that acquiring and maintaining talent will remain one of the most difficult difficulties in 2022. We will need to be flexible, transparent, and agile as leaders in how we approach these challenges and opportunities, whether it's recruiting talent, developing products and services, preparing for new risks and regulations, or inspiring and motivating employees so that they and the organisation can grow and thrive. Where do you anticipate compliance initiatives heading in the future?

Compliance affects all departments, whether you work in human resources or benefits, finance, information technology, buying, or sales and marketing, and all workers must understand what to do (and what not to do) to identify risks, prevent infractions, and safeguard the organisation's reputation.

How should businesses evaluate compliance training programs? Do you notice businesses taking a more proactive approach to training?

During the COVID-19 outbreak, fraud has been extremely problematic. People have been focused on purchasing basic things since there has been a noticeable reduction in consumption. With the events of the COVID-19, unethical behaviour in the workplace has increased. I polled a group of business executives to find out what the most frequent ethical problems are in today's organisations.

More businesses are discovering that compliance training is neither a one-size-fits-all solution nor a checkbox item. They want training to be relevant to their employees and to be part of a multi-pronged strategy to foster an ethical and compliant culture. Regardless of whether employees are stationed onsite, remotely, or in a hybrid situation, training should reflect today's developing work environment and what it means to "do the right thing." Effective compliance training promotes a "speak up" culture, which encourages and facilitates employees raising concerns and reporting violations. Here are four questions to ask while considering compliance training: Is your workers' and supervisors' training relevant? Is it possible to tailor it to your company's industry, culture, brand, and internal regulations and procedures?

It is not just vital that training be current with your organisation's policies, practises, and procedures. Is the training current? Not only must training be current with your organisation's policies, procedures, and new laws and regulations, but material must also be kept fresh so that employees aren't taking the same course year after year. Is the training based on behavior? Rather than focusing on liability avoidance, successful training should concentrate on modifying attitudes, boosting understanding of what is and isn't proper workplace behaviour, and the repercussions of wrongdoing. Employees will continue to look to leadership for clear advice, comfort, and assistance at a time of uncertainty in 2022. Developing a solid foundation of ethics and compliance may aid in the development of trust, encourage honest criticism, and enable workers to bring their complete selves to work. However, the most thought provoking questions are:

- Have major expenditures and enhancements been made to the organisation's compliance programme and internal control systems?
- Have the compliance program's corrective measures been evaluated to demonstrate that they will prevent future misconduct?
- Are there methods in place for workers to report claims of a breach of the organisation's code of conduct or other wrongdoing anonymously or confidentially?
- Is the training engaging learners with relevant examples, interactive scenarios, and practical activities that they can put into action right away?

"When assessing overall compliance procedures, organisations should look to important components of the my piece of advice is excellence in compliance and conscientiousness fosters a stronger organisational culture. Successful organisations have many characteristics, including sustainable and resilient business processes and exceptional customer service, which is frequently accompanied by high-quality products and services. A strong, ethics-centered culture lies at the heart of these behaviours."

-Dr. Amit Das

CHAPTER TWO

A Business Without Value Is A Business At Risk

"If people are good only because they fear punishment, and hope for reward, then we are a sorry lot indeed." -Albert Einstein

In today's economic world, moral and ethical leadership are critical. It is critical to have a system in place to ensure ethical behaviour at all levels. Ethical and moral leadership are also included in the social responsibility area. This is about doing what is right and moral in the eyes of the public, as well as having a plan in place to ensure ethical decision-making. It is critical to have a leader who is truthful, not only to himself but also to others.

"When a leader is truthful, the organisation gains a sense of transparency and, as a result, trust."

The best way to be honest with employees and establish confidence is to provide facts up front to the organisation about why these layoffs are occurring and strategies to reorganise roles to either maintain jobs or fill unfilled positions. Cost-cutting tactics with in an organisation are an example. Stakeholders include everyone in the organisation. Everyone has a stake in the company, from employees to consumers.

It is critical to have an open dialogue with employees in order to support ethical behaviour. According to leaders, profits must not come before stakeholders. This does not imply that the organisation is deliberately losing money. Obviously, the organisation exists to generate a profit. This implies that choices must be made with the best interests of all parties in mind. A sales company, for example, could increase its sales force's annual targets. The objectives are unachievable, and no one receives a bonus. This may result in employee dissatisfaction and mistrust.

Adjusting goals and increasing bonus payouts are the correct steps to take to enhance employee motivation. Everyone in an organisation is working toward a common objective if the leader creates a feeling of community. Take, for example, a pharmaceutical firm. The organisation's overall objective is to generate a profit. The leader's first priority, however, must be to communicate that the patient comes first and that the treatment will benefit the patient. Profits will follow if the drug benefits the patient. The group will develop a feeling of community if the leader establishes a shared aim. It is critical for leaders to operate morally and ethically in today's corporate world. This provides workers with internal transparency and fosters a sense of trust in the organisation's executives.

"A leader is responsible for creating an organisation that resembles a close-knit community."

The organisation can function as a cohesive entity that acts ethically by having its leaders act ethically and having a plan to ensure ethical leadership. The moral and ethical leader does not market himself or herself as ethical. The moral and ethical leader sets an example for others to follow. They also carry out socially responsible details. They do things behind the scenes that go unseen yet are crucial to their success as ethical leaders.

Traditional corporate leadership styles have simply paid lip service to controlling the social context in which businesses function up until now. Today's company leaders may be losing out on a wonderful chance to "future-proof" their organisations by utilising new digitised technology to build workplaces where people flourish because their social requirements are addressed.

What is the definition of ethical leadership?

Many people see that today's traditional business structures are out of step with major technological advancements that have dissolved corporate borders and connected suppliers and customers into a sharing economy, whether it's Uber, Airbnb, or crowdfunding. Many businesses' success is being sabotaged by old methods of thinking and doing. The new ethical leadership paradigm that requires employees to release discretionary effort differs significantly from previous models. It prioritises employees and produces results as a result of their degrees of involvement. Despite this, annual employee engagement surveys show that CEOs are hesitant to actively and purposefully construct their company's culture.

"At its best, leadership development is not an "event." It's a capacity-building endeavor. It's a process of human growth and development."-Linda Fisher Thornton

It's all about instilling the appropriate habits. It's all about doing the right thing when faced with a problem. We can see the behaviour that happens, but we can't see the values that lead to that behaviour. Values are the unseen forces that influence our actions. They have an impact on our views, and our attitudes have an impact on our ethical behaviour. An ethical behavioural chain is formed by the relationship between values, attitudes, and behaviour. It is critical to recognise that the first stage of ethical leadership is to establish the ethical tone from the top in order to shape the desired employee behaviours in the organisation.

It's more critical than ever to ensure that, as a leader, your ethical message is consistent in today's high-visibility environment with the continual social media onslaught. Anyone may walk the talk, but if you don't sincerely believe in the value of ethical behaviour in your professional life, it will show to your colleagues, peers, and the individuals in the C-suite.

> ***"Ethical leadership entails corporate executives acting ethically both within and outside of the workplace."***

According to the HBR, ethical leaders will not overlook misconduct even if it is beneficial to their companies. Integrity and doing the right thing are keys to becoming an ethical leader. Ethical leaders serve as role models for the rest of the organisation. To be an ethical leader, you must act ethically all of the time and throughout time, not only while others are watching. Doing the right thing all of the time, especially when it's tough, should be ingrained in a leader's DNA. It's unavoidable that you'll be found out if you act ethically in public yet evade responsibilities, cut costs, and prioritise business above people behind closed doors.

In modern times, corporate indiscretion, malfeasance, and deviance are constantly in the news and all around us. There isn't a day that goes by without news of a new organisational flaw. Organisations in every sector of society, both in India and throughout the world, consistently disappoint and frustrate us in terms of ethical grandeur. Much of what we view as the shadow or dark side of organisational behaviour is frequently difficult to grasp and appreciate. It baffles me how extremely committed, conscientious, and skilled middle-level executives or astute, successful, and powerful CEOs can cross the line and do such stupid things that jeopardise their jobs, wealth, reputation, families, and careers.

Too many organisations' ideals are unoperationalised, and their cultures are dysfunctional due to a lack of managerial consistency. Thankfully, ethical leadership is not the same as ordinary leadership. You may anticipate new workers continuing to vote with their feet and quit their companies after 1 or 2 years in pursuit of more rewarding work if leaders fail to adopt the new ethical leadership paradigm.

Organisations now operate in a highly competitive and dynamic environment, which forces them to alter their organisational structures on a regular basis. However, the success of change programs may be hampered by employee resistance, particularly if they are unprepared to change. While ethical leaders who serve as guides and give support can help boost workers' readiness to change, ethical leaders who serve as guides and offer support can also make a difference by lowering ambiguity. However, there is virtually little study on the function of ethical leadership in improving employees' willingness to change.

The behaviour or response of a leader in any particular event has an impact on future organisational behaviour in comparable situations, either strengthening or weakening its overall ethical substance. For example, if a high-performing employee cheats on the cost account and the boss overlooks it because of the person's good performance, the employee's desire to cheat will be increased. Employees, in particular, want to be led by people who have a moral operating system that is based on stated principles. Over time, this approach has become a model of ethics for the whole corporation. It is vital that the reaction of the individual leader be consistent with his or her championed ideals, morally grounded procedures, and declared behavioural standards. Actions speak louder than words in ethics, and they generate a buzz at the intermediate and junior levels. Value-centered reactions that are consistent help to foster ethical organisational behaviour. Established behavioural standards also aid in highlighting those areas that a leader wishes to emphasise as crucial in building a pattern of ethical behaviour based on the existing ethical state of the organisation.

In terms of the second driver, ethical behaviour, a thorough ethics program is required to improve organisational members' ethical behaviour. The essential parts of an ethics program include: evaluation of the organisation's underlying beliefs and philosophies; conformity with the organisation's structures, procedures, and policies; and fulfilment of senior leadership's ethical goals. Based on these essentials, an ethics curriculum with the following elements can be built: Is this correct?

A formal ethical code; the formation of an ethics committee; the appointment of an ethics officer; an ethics communication system; an ethics training program; and a system for tracking and managing consequences. The term "code of ethics" refers to a written declaration of an organisation's permitted range of behaviours and acts. It consists of a written set of guidelines that must be followed by executives and other employees. A board-level ethics committee should be created to oversee how ethicallyan organisation conducts its operations and to indicate that ethical issues are taken seriously. The duty of overseeing the ethics program might then be entrusted to a specialised employee chosen specifically for the task.

Hence, ethics is all about communication and education. Hence, other elements like ethics, communication, and training systems are important. Furthermore, a proper system for transgressors' repercussions management should be put in place.

Do you feel that leadership skills should be a significant priority for organisational learning?

Certainly, leadership skills should be a significant priority for learning, which should not be misconstrued as being offered primarily for leadership and management jobs. Instead, all workers in a human-centered organisation should be taught to see leadership as an activity for everyone rather than a personality attribute, and they should be appropriately upskilled in strategies to enhance teaching—by establishing a learning atmosphere—and empathy. Human-centered organisations are ideally positioned to maximise the effectiveness of any change proposition by leading with empathy at all levels of the organisation. This is because it organically considers and places individuals participating in the change process at the centre of any future dialogue, design, or strategy.

Businesses may better access the expert voices they need to make effective changes and generate buy-in from the people they need to deliver them by building an open, trustworthy, and compassionate workplace. The epidemic taught us that connections are everything and that we are capable of extraordinary feats. Weaving people into the heart of our organisations inevitably leads to happier, healthier, and more engaged workforces. These are the people who will go above and beyond foran organisation because they feel their contribution is valued and realise that every employee contributes to the company's overall moral goal. These organisations will prosper through unleashing human potential in service of all of our futures.

New leadership, like new culture, can modify the notion of loyalty, but until we set a standard for this, rewarding "loyal conduct" will be difficult. Consider two employees who have comparable positions and experiences, but one has worked three years longer than the other and prefers to go the additional mile. Who would you honor? Or, if they both receive market offers, who would be your first choice to keep? Workplace culture has been put to the test during the last two years. In a remote or hybrid work setting, how well didan organisation's values and purpose hold up? Some groups passed with flying colours, while others did not. The set of rules and procedures put in place by an employer, as well as the training programmes established to reinforce them, are at the heart of the problem. Organisations that have established a strong foundation of ethics and compliance are better positioned to not just survive but grow as we deal with the aftermath of the epidemic.

What have been some of the most significant ethical and compliance changes and problems for organisations in recent years?

The COVID-19 epidemic has altered the way we conduct business, causing disruptions in everything from global supply networks to financial markets. Two years from now, when business models are changed and rebuilt, the finance department will be at the centre of this transformation. This is applicable not just to companies that went online during the epidemic but also to those that went offline when they digitised their accounting and tax compliance or began taking digital payments. Most business owners and laypeople regard compliance as either tedious or amazing. even as Indian company owners witness a major seismic shift in the compliance landscape. It is a creative and strong integration to establish a slew of watchdogs to ensure compliance with the government and quasi-governmental agencies such as the National Stock Exchange (NSE), which penalises around 250 corporations for non-compliance with laws. This implies that the cost of noncompliance may exceed the cost of compliance.

Leaders are aware of their influence on others and are concerned about it. They pay attention to others, are accepting of differing viewpoints, and treat people as ends in themselves, never as a means to a purpose. Leaders have a responsibility to serve and lead in a servant-like manner. They put the interests of others ahead of their own and act in ways that benefit others. They are concerned about others' well-being and engage in activities such as mentorship, empowerment, and team building. A leader who establishes a common vision for an effort by first doing a "listening tour" to determine what his people require and value for.

- When making decisions, leaders prioritise fairness and justice, which includes exhibiting fairness to individuals as well as the greater society.
- When it comes to hiring employees, setting salaries, or selecting external service providers, they must insist on fair and transparent methods.
- They display honesty and integrity, which aids in the development of trust, the strengthening of relationships, and the development of personal authority.

- They are also open and honest in their contacts with others, as well as diplomatic and understanding of others' needs.
- They also stick to their obligations. A leader who admits to making a mistake and accepts responsibility for it is.

A leader who recognisess an opportunity to solve a greater, broader societal problem by addressing a local problem that directly affects them and joins with other leaders to establish an effort that helps the broader community. In recent years, you've heard a lot about compassionate leadership, but 2020-21 has been a true test of how organisations can combine it with ethical leadership. Being an ethical leader entails more than merely declaring your intention to behave in the best interests of everybody.

Jack Ma's attitude on the subject has been quite strict, including terminating employees who may have engaged in unethical behavior. "If we terminate them right away, the firm will lose money." What does this say about us if we don't fire these employees? It would indicate that our words are meaningless. So we eventually made the decision to let these two individuals go.

Make an active strategy for how your job behaviour may help you become a more ethical leader. If you make a commitment, you will go to great lengths to maintain it. Through training opportunities, ethical behaviour should constantly be stressed. Schedule workshops that emphasize the importance of treating people ethically in the workplace. Be open and honest in all business transactions.

If your organisation has to shrink, for example, notify employees well in advance. More than ideals are required for ethical leadership. Care, justice, honesty, and respect are the raw materials of ethical leadership, but you must be transformed into effective acts in complicated and dynamic settings through a manufacturing process.

As a result, you can deduce that ethical leaders adhere to what may be universal values such as fairness, equality, and respect, and extend these leadership principles beyond the business context. Furthermore, ethical leaders strive for it!!

Warren Buffet has witnessed the birth of some of the world's most recognised brands and enterprises, including Apple, Costco, IBM, and others. He has a keen eye for environmentally friendly company methods. Buffet's attitude toward ethics is not about virtue signalling; rather, it is about good financial sense. He believes that nothing impacts the lifespan of a brand.

Elon Musk is one of the world's wealthiest people, with a net worth of more than $221 billion as of March, 2022, and is regarded as an innovator, with initiatives like Tesla, SpaceX, and the Hyperloop, among others. Musk has donated millions of dollars to charitable organisations and has his own foundation, the Musk Foundation, which has helped with hurricane and tsunami relief, as well as the Future of Life Institute, which aims to ensure that future artificial intelligence applications are beneficial to humanity.

Ethical leadership necessitates the presence of ethical leaders. Leaders that are ethical may guarantee that ethical practises are followed across the company. Because leaders are inherently in a position of authority both on and off the job, ethical leadership must concentrate on how they use that power in their decisions, actions, and ways of influencing others.

Leaders are in charge of persuading followers to do specific acts, accomplish tasks, and act in certain ways. As they support the internalisation of the corporate vision, effective leaders also influence processes, inspire change in attitudes and values, and enhance the empowerment and self-efficacy of their followers. The nurturing part of leadership may also help to boost an organisation's culture and employee values to more ethical levels.

As a result, ethical leadership linked to ideas like trust, honesty, thoughtfulness, charm, and justice. Except for the introduction of charm, much of this is logic. Ethical leaders don't need charisma; in fact, data reveals that many charismatic leaders have persuaded their followers to abandon their principles and convictions. Even more concerning is the reality that history is littered with charismatic leaders who rank poorly on the scale of ethical leadership.

You foster a high degree of integrity by exhibiting ethical leadership, which promotes a sense of trustworthiness and inspires subordinates to embrace and follow our vision. Other personal attributes that guide your ethical ideas, attitudes, and judgments are founded on character and integrity. Ethical leaders are likely to be people-oriented and conscious of the consequences of their decisions.

As a result, you use your influence and authority to serve the greater good rather than self-serving goals, resulting in a "win/win" situation for both employees and the company. This role modelling acts as a guide and motivation for others to prioritise the group's needs and interests over your own.

What are the distinctive characteristics of ethical leaders?

- Fairness is practised by ethical leaders by ensuring that everyone is treated fairly and equitably.
- Ethical leaders adhere to a set of consistent, widely held values or principles, such as honesty, fairness, respect, caring for others, accountability for one's actions, prioritizing the greater good over one's personal interests, and so on.
- Ethical leaders encourage ethical behaviour in the workplace and prohibit unethical behavior. Ethical leaders incorporate ethical considerations into their decision-making processes.
- Ethical leaders accept responsibility for both their successes and failures.

- They respect others, which is one of the characteristics of an ethical leader. An ethical leader should not use his or her followers to attain personal objectives.
- They are servant to others. An ethical leader should prioritise the needs of his followers before his own. They should be compassionate.
- They are just and fair. Wherever certain followers are treated differently, the basis for such treatment should be fair, transparent, and moral.
- They foster community. An ethical leader thinks about his own objectives as well as the aspirations of his followers and strives to attain goals that are beneficial to both. He puts forth more effort to achieve the community's objectives.
- They are dependable and trustworthy. Honest leaders may be trusted and counted on at all times. They consistently gain the respect of their fans.
- Individual respect implies that the leader respects everyone's moral standards. Nobody's values are

superior or inferior to anybody else's. The leader may build confidence in an organisation by valuing the individual. The golden rule comes to mind as the best example: treat others the way you want to be treated. If a leader respects himself or herself, he or she will respect others.

- Effective communication is essential for ethical leadership.
- Ethical standards should be clearly stated and individuals should be aware of them.
- Even when painful judgments must be made, the decision-making process should be publicly shared.
- Ethics should be addressed not only in times of crisis or major decision-making, but also in day-to-day operations.
- The leader must be able to build strong bonds with his or her followers. These connections must be built on the foundations of trust, respect, and open communication.
- Ethical leadership should be more inclusive of ethics.
- Organisations should think about doing the right thing not simply in terms of following the rules, but also in terms of social justice and sustainability.
- Everyone on the team should be aware of the framework and the significance of ethical behavior, and they should act accordingly.
- Rather than focusing on what ethical leadership should not be, the emphasis should be on developing and enforcing the appropriate model and framework for ethical leadership.
- Ethical leaders take their jobs seriously and wish to be successful in them.
- They also wish to assist in the empowerment of others and guarantee the success of the company and

subordinates they serve.

- The ethical leader emphasises the importance of hard work and devotion in completing the task.
- An ethical leader aspires to be defined and thought of as a decent person. There is a worry about doing the right thing and, maybe more crucially, thinking about what the appropriate action is.
- Ethical leaders are welcoming to everybody. This indicates that they are receptive to other viewpoints and encourage employees to share their thoughts. But, in addition to this kind of communicative and collaborative inclusion, ethical leaders interact with individuals from all walks of life.
- An ethical leader recognizess the value of a diverse workplace and strives to make the organisation more inclusive of people of many nationalities, colours, cultures, and backgrounds.
- An ethical leader will talk about the high ideals and standards they have for themselves, their team, and the organisation on a frequent basis.

Knowing your underlying principles and having the guts to follow them in all aspects of your life in the service of the greater good is what ethical leadership entails. In my view, ethical leadership means leading in a way that respects others' rights and dignity, a concept that might be at odds with more traditional leadership paradigms. The major purpose of leadership in the past was to boost production and profitability. However, in the twenty-first century, this viewpoint has begun to fade as more organisational development and human resources professionals say that leaders are equally responsible for upholding moral and ethical norms. Therefore, good leadership entails not just ability but also ethics that alter companies and people's lives.

What are the challenges faced by ethical laeders?

For today's leaders, ethical leadership is critical. The significance of being ethical in business and in life has been highlighted by the news in recent months and years. So, what can you do to make sure you're a principled leader who's building an ethical company? Begin by having an open conversation with your leadership team, assisting them in discovering and claiming their fundamental values, and then working together to construct a vision for how your world may be different using the 3-V Model. The 3-V Model of Ethical Leadership as a framework for aligning leaders' internal beliefs and values with their exterior behaviours and actions for the greater good of workers, leaders, companies, and society.

- Vision: Ethical leadership necessitates the capacity to frame our activities inside an image of "what should be"—especially when it comes to serving others.
- Voice: Ethical leaders must be able to convey their vision to others in a genuine way that motivates people to take action. Ethical leaders try to do the correct and good things.
- Virtue: Ethical leaders demonstrate virtue by asking themselves, "How do my values, vision, and voice match with and promote the common good?"Owners, the C Suite, and senior management should create an atmosphere in which people have the discipline and strength to regularly select virtue; virtue will then become a habit that will get stronger with practise.

What was once widely acknowledged as good and true, just and just, is now a point of contention. It is extremely difficult for values-based leaders to thrive in an atmosphere of relativism. Starting from the top down is the only way to develop an ethical business. Your workers will pick up on your actions, decisions, and ideals and apply them to their own work.

Leading by example instils respect and shows your employees that you believe in them and are confident in their abilities. As the expression goes, you can't pour from an empty cup. Leaders who look after themselves are more likely to manage and care for others effectively.

As a leader, you will undoubtedly face difficulties. The way you cope with and overcome these obstacles shapes who you are as people and the image you project to others. your "moral values" determine how you as individuals display a code of behaviour that is acceptable and suitable.

Ethical leadership means examining your moral values and how you apply them in your daily lives. This shows your leadership beliefs and successes. You can accept responsibility for your decisions and comprehend the necessity of openness if you are able to accept accountability for your decisions. Consider this scenario: you've been asked to make a game-changing decision that makes you feel uneasy. Your job is on the line, and if you don't make a choice, you may lose it. You know from a slew of studies that ethically-driven decision-making and leadership foster credibility, respect, process, motives, and trust, as well as a positive environment in which employees, customers, and suppliers engage in profitable long-term relationships that benefit all stakeholders.

Of course, psychopathic narcissists can benefit in the short run; just look at Bernard Madoff's case. His Ponzi scheme fell apart after years of "ripping people off" and living an incredibly luxurious life, and he was sentenced to a number of lifetimes in jail for his immoral conduct. Although the German carmaker has a history of cultivating a competitive corporate culture, Martin Winterkorn, the company's CEO since 2007, may have contributed to a culture that allowed the installation of software that failed to correctly detect emissions on its vehicles. Winterkorn appears to have been renowned as a hard-driving perfectionist who would go about with a gauge in his hand to measure gaps between vehicle doors in his tireless quest for the top rank among global auto makers, despite his claims that he was unaware of the misconduct. Bad actions, motivated by the need for immediate gratification, frequently result in unfavourable long-term consequences. Being a long-term business leader who is ethical is also the most effective strategy to defend and growan organisation. You've been monitoring headlines about British Home Stores, Toyota, Rolls-Royce, BT, Samsung, Toshiba, Toyota, and a variety of other corporations in recent months, and you've been wondering where all the ethically-driven corporate executives have gone.

Your personal-promotion of conduct to your people through effective two-way communication, encouragement of excellent behaviour, and reflecting your beliefs through your decision-making are all examples of ethical leadership. By accepting responsibility for your decisions and realising the significance of transparency, you motivate people to follow your lead. To become this style of leader, you must analyse your values, thoughts, and objectives honestly.

Ethical leaders who take responsibility for this have a greater understanding of how their own activities influence and impact others. Understanding the significance of a cultural framework that others gladly follow creates a successful platform. Individuals may better grasp the influence of corrective behaviour, both individually and at work, by educating people about prevalent ethical challenges occurring throughout the world, governance frameworks, and other significant elements. Now, there are a number of business endeavours and things going on that aren't ready for public consumption, if you will, and you must respect that because stories circulate and things may get out of hand. As a result, you won't always be able to share everything. Discarding something because of the character of the person who could deliver it to you is a very, very dangerous trap.

So, it's easy to get caught up in your day-to-day work as a leader and forget about these traps. People are where ethics may be found. In truth, the organisation's ethics are represented by its leaders. The majority of businesses have a set of codified ethical guidelines. And although that gives advice, and it's a wonderful thing that it does, whatever conduct emanates from the organisation's executives symbolises the organisation's ethics. Every leader, at some time, will fall into an ethical trap. The first is attempting to soften the shock of terrible news or prospective bad news by lying or coming dangerously close to lying as a result. Let me give you an illustration. Let's imagine your organisation is going through a cost-cutting or resource-allocation process, or whatever phrase you choose to use.

Given the macro-changes influencing your society, the demand for ethical leadership will grow in the next few years. Leaders in most industries will encounter complexity, fast change, fierce competition, globalization, disruption, and new technologies in the near future.

Leaders will need to handle ethical difficulties around hard subjects like artificial intelligence, managing people's private data, robots, and genetic engineering, to mention a few, in this context.

As a result, you still have a long way to go in terms of closing the gap between existing practise and the capacity you'll need in the near future in terms of ethical leadership. Leaders and followers form an intellectual and emotional bond as a result of such involvement, making both sides equally accountable in the pursuit of mutual goals. Cohorts are also coached by ethical leaders in developing a sense of personal and professional competence, which helps them thrive while also being more resilient, loyal, and lucrative. Employees look up to morally-minded role models where and when they see them at work. There is a strong link between a personally motivated moral conscience, business ethics, and long-term company success.

Would you like to check on your ethical leadership skills ?

Leaders who are successful add value. As an ethical leader, embracing ownership and accountability for adding value is critical to your personal and organisational success. Having a strong commitment to establishing a communication flow and leading by example will foster loyalty and productivity. You're confident that the majority of you can think of a few immoral decisions.

- You exhibit a strong dedication to ethical and moral ideals.
- You communicate ethical standards to members in a clear and concise manner.
- You Set an example of ethical behaviour in your decisions and behavior.

- You are trustworthy and can be relied upon to tell the truth.
- You acts on your stated values "walk the talk".
- You distribute work to members in a fair and impartial manner.
- You can be counted on to keep promises and obligations.
- You are adamant about doing what is right and fair, even when it is difficult.
- You recognise and accept responsibility for mistakes made.
- You believe that honesty and integrity are important personal qualities for ethical leaders.
- You lead by example in terms of devotion and self-sacrifice for the company.
- You disapprove of the use of unethical methods to improve performance.
- When evaluating member performance and awarding awards, it is fair and objective.
- You put the needs of others ahead of your own.
- Your team members are held accountable for adhering to ethical standards in their work.

"Effective leaders focus on what's right and exemplify to their people that they are there to help, and not to exploit the vulnerabilities of others. Their organisations typically respond to their example and their desire to serve others and make a positive difference."

It is the responsibility of an ethical leader to communicate with each team member while also allowing for free discussion, since some people may have questions or concerns that need to be addressed. Ethical leaders who set a good example may inspire others to follow suit. People are generally influenced by the interactions that take place around them. Positive coworker communication may have an impact on workplace productivity and attitude.

Ethical leaders may contribute to the creation of a pleasant atmosphere with constructive interactions on three levels: the person, the team, and the company as a whole. Ethical leadership can also include managing a team's behaviour and collaboration. A strong ethical leader's role includes maintaining a pleasant work environment.

"Ethical leaders collaborate and develop succession plans for their organisations to ensure the organisation's long-term prosperity."

Instead of continually re-thinking and assessing the issue, an ethical framework assists a leader and the company in making decisions and approaching activities with a cohesive strategy. Although a framework will not always provide ethical leaders with a clear answer, it will make it simpler to assess the circumstances and listen to other people's perspectives on the subject.

What values are motivating decision-making in companies as they navigate uncertain times ahead?

With what has unfolded before us in 2020, the importance of ethical leadership has never been greater. This year has been particularly difficult for airlines and hotels, and you can look to the sector for another wonderful example of ethical leadership from the former CEO of Japan Airlines. Haruka Nishimatsu was a CEO who rode the bus to work and ate lunch with his coworkers in the office canteen. He didn't hide in the ivory towers; instead, he made himself available to his whole team. When things were rough a decade ago, he accepted a substantial wage cut to earn less than his pilots. If his employees had to suffer, he made sure he did as well. Kazuo Inamori,

Nishimatsu's replacement, went one step further by refusing to take a salary while successfully turning JAL into a profitable airline.

A leader motivates and encourages his or her subordinates and followers to work together to achieve a shared objective, whether it's teamwork, corporate goals, or a project. Because everyone of his subordinates has a distinct personality, it is the leader's ethical responsibility to treat them with respect. Because leaders hold a significant position in the organisation and have an impact on the development of organisational values, they shape and develop the ethical environment.

In today's business, defining employee loyalty via mindset alignment provided a variety of perspectives on the issue. However, the overwhelming feeling was that tenure did not imply loyalty. Instead, the most common characteristics were strong dedication and tenacity through the organisation's peaks and valleys, persistent value generation, care for the organisation, and ownership of labor.

Ethical leadership is a management approach that may be applied to any company. The following are the most significant advantages for an organisation that values ethical leadership:

- When employees work for an ethical boss, their morale rises.
- Employees will not feel as though they are assisting a crooked individual in accumulating even more wealth.
- Ethical leaders have the ability to motivate others who work with them to achieve their full potential.
- Ethical executives do not harman organisation's reputation.

- Company scandals can harman organisation's reputation and drive consumers to switch to a rival.
- Companies that appoint ethical executives are more likely to retain both employees and consumers.

As a result, it is linked to ideas like trust, honesty, thoughtfulness, charm, and justice. Ethical leadership is a type of leadership in which people act in a way that is acceptable and suitable for the greater good in all aspects of their lives.

Ethical leadership is a leadership paradigm that applies the aforementioned ethical ideals to the management of subordinates. Because ethics is concerned with the principles of "good" behaviour and leadership is concerned with persuading others to attain a goal, ethical leadership is influencing others via ethics. People are more prone to assessing others based on their actions than their words.

Ethical leaders may acquire the respect of their peers by exercising and displaying ethical, honest, and selfless behaviour towards their subordinates. People are more inclined to follow a leader who is trustworthy and respects others.

If you expect your employees to treat everyone with respect, you can't expect them to take you seriously if you make fun of them or gossip about them. If you're prepared to break the rules for the sake of convenience, the same applies. If your company is compelled to follow federal and state rules, for example, your employees will be upset if labour standards or environmental restrictions are broken. Employees will pick up on your hypocrisy and regard your company's goal and vision as a public façade.

Ethics is a difficult subject. You must develop clear policies in the form of mission statements, rules, laws, and practices to ensure clarity. Employees require written copies of the following policies from the moment they are employed. These must also be documented in an easy-to-understand manner that is devoid of exploitable flaws. If you're stuck for ideas, consider basing your company's vision and policies on the visions and policies of other organisations that you admire or find successful. You may also engage a consultant to examine your company and recommend the best course of action. The culture and atmosphere of the workplace can also pose a threat to ethical leadership. When faced with moral grey zones, ethical leadership may be extremely tough. In situations like these, doing the right thing may be counterproductive to your company's financial line. You're ready to grow, but new safety standards mandate that you replace the organisation's equipment, which will cost you money. You can reason that your present equipment is acceptable and that breaking the laws in this one instance would enhance profits and allow you to hire additional people in the community. To put it another way, the ends justify the methods.

However, if an injured worker sues you after learning that you deliberately disobeyed safety standards, you might face major legal trouble. An ethical leader recognises that an organisation's worldwide market competitiveness is determined by three factors: quality product, quality customer service, and quality delivery.

How to become an ethical leader?

The role of ethical leadership must be taken seriously and with respect. As previously said, you may demonstrate real ethical leadership and so develop confidence among your subordinates by doing what you say. As a leader, you must take responsibility for your actions and decisions. An ethical leader must think about all of his or her activities and figure out how to do the least amount of harm possible. Ethical leaders will frequently be confronted with circumstances in which both actions have the potential to bring good or harm, but they must be mindful of picking the "best" response for the scenario while keeping in mind their general ethical framework and the organisation's purpose.

In order to be ethical, a leader must be consistent in his or her approach. By adhering to his or her own ethical standards, an ethical leader can encourage his or her employees. You must also be consistent in your treatment of subordinates and stakeholders. When dealing with others, you must lay forth the norms and ethical framework and adhere to them. You can't scold someone for doing something you wouldn't do in a different scenario. Leaders who are ethical must learn to be authoritative and to leverage their influence.

However, there are significant differences between how autocratic or authoritarian leaders use authority and how ethical leaders manage their employees. Whereas more authoritarian leadership approaches place decision-making in the hands of the leader, ethical leadership requires teamwork. It does not imply that the ethical leader would not make the ultimate choice; rather, it suggests that power is organised in such a manner that others can share it with the leader. It should go without saying that someone who is ethical is also trustworthy and loyal. Within the organisation, ethical leaders build a feeling of community and team spirit.

When an ethical leader sets out to achieve goals, it's not simply about achieving personal objectives. Because followers trust honest and trustworthy leaders, being honest is especially vital for becoming an effective ethical leader. A moral leader is always kind and fair. They don't play favourites and treat everyone the same. No employee should be afraid of being treated unfairly because of their gender, race, nationality, or any other factor under the leadership of an ethical leader. Respect for followers is one of the most crucial characteristics of ethical leadership. Employees grow and develop under the leadership of an ethical leader. Employees are rewarded for coming up with novel ideas and encouraged to go above and above to enhance how things are done. Employees are commended for taking the initiative rather than waiting for someone else to do it. All choices made by ethical leaders are double-checked to verify that they are in line with the organisation's overarching principles. Only those choices that match this requirement are implemented.

Ethical leadership is more than simply talking the talk; it also entails doing the walk. The high expectations that an ethical leader has for his or her employees also apply to individuals. By leading by example, leaders expect others to follow suit. They guarantee that there is uniform knowledge across the organisation by communicating and debating values on a regular basis. Employees who work under an ethical leader are expected to do the right thing all of the time, not just when it is convenient for them.

Individuals communicate in a variety of ways. Others may be afraid to talk with a leader because of fear, anxiety, or just not understanding how to explain what they are attempting to say in public, regardless of who they are dealing with or the scenario. As an ethical leader, it's critical to teach others about ethics, especially when they're confronted with an ethical dilemma at work. One responsibility of an ethical leader is to focus on the general relevance of ethics, including ethical standards and other ethical challenges, and how these elements might impact society. It is critical for leaders to foster camaraderie among their employees. Trust, fairness, honesty, openness, compassion, and respect are all qualities that characterize good partnerships. It's easy to lose sight of what your firm stands for as your company expands.

As your organisation grows, it might be tough to guarantee that all of your employees obey the rules and embody your company's goal, vision, and values. Understanding how to overcome some of the obstacles to ethical leadership can not only helps you preserve goodwill with the public and stakeholders, but it may also help you avoid future difficulties.

One of the most difficult aspects of ethical leadership is the ability to stick to the rules you set for your company. Following your own ethical code serves as an example to your employees, demonstrating that you are committed to them. Following your own ethical code inspires your colleagues by demonstrating that you are committed to your fundamental beliefs.

Ethics-based leadership techniques such as genuine and ethical leadership had similar associations with a wide range of positive employee outcomes as transformational leadership (e.g., trust in supervisor, engagement, and job satisfaction). Furthermore, their meta-analytic study discovered that the more emphasis leaders place on ethics, the better their ability to predict positive outcomes. They also found that ethical leadership is significantly positively related to employee task performance, even in the presence of transformational leadership. As a result, ethical leadership may have a role to play in anticipating a valued outcome in the workplace, such as willingness to change, which has been practically untapped until now.

Finally, ethical leadership entails corporate executives acting ethically both within and outside of the workplace. Being an ethical leader entails more than merely declaring your intention to behave in the best interests of everybody. Ethical leaders are likely to be people-oriented and conscious of the consequences of their decisions. Ethical leaders encourage ethical behaviour in the workplace and prohibit unethical behavior. Leading by example instils respect and shows your employees that you believe in them and are confident in their abilities. Every leader, at some time, will fall into an ethical trap. Ethical leaders have a greater understanding of how their own activities influence and impact others. One of the most difficult aspects of ethical leadership is the ability to stick to the rules you set for your company. Following your own ethical code inspires your colleagues by demonstrating that you are committed to your fundamental beliefs. Ethical leadership may have a role to play in anticipating a valued outcome in the workplace, such as willingness to change.

"Organisations' practises and policies are intended to have a positive influence on the world."

Organisations must follow and comprehend all applicable local, national, and international laws and regulations, as well as all written, stated, and enforced laws and regulations, in line with established, specialised processes. The firm must declare its policies, choices, and operations in a clear, accurate, and complete manner, including any known or possible consequences for the environment and society.

Do you agree that corporate social responsibility aims to enhance communities, the economy, and the environment?

CSR has been the subject of several discussions and studies over the last few years. It has become more important in both academic and corporate circles. It encompasses a wide range of ideals and criteria for assessingan organisation's social impact. Many related and overlapping ideas, including corporate citizenship, business ethics, stakeholder management, and sustainability, have evolved as a result of the constant usage of the word "CSR." Multiple views and by those in supporting positions such as the business sector, government agencies, academia, and the public sector are indicated by the wide range of synonymously used terminology.

- CSR is a sort of self-regulation practised by businesses with the goal of becoming socially responsible. It enables businesses to assess their influence on all parts of society, including economic, social, and environmental factors.
- CSR refers to an organisation's decision to operate in ways that benefit society and the environment rather than harm them.
- CSR is an organisation strategy that promotes long-term growth by providing economic, social, and environmental benefits to all stakeholders.
- CSR is a broad topic with several meanings and applications. Each firm and nation has its own manner of understanding and implementing it.
- Furthermore, CSR is a broad term that encompasses a wide range of issues, including human rights, corporate governance, health and safety, environmental impacts, working conditions, and economic growth.
- CSR refers toan organisation's activities and policies that benefit the environment, the economy, and society.

Customers, suppliers, shareholders, and workers, as well as the government, have their demands met.

- Whatever definition is used, the goal of CSR is to promote change that leads to long-term sustainability.
- CSR refers to how a corporation balances economic, environmental, and social goals while also meeting stakeholder expectations and maintaining or increasing shareholder value.
- CSR refers to an organisation's total connection with its stakeholders, which includes customers, workers, communities, owners/investors, the government, suppliers, and rivals. Investment in community outreach, employee relations, job development and retention, environmental responsibility, and financial success are all examples of CSR.
- CSR is a term that refers to company actions that help society. CSR can include a range of strategies, such as donating a percentage ofan organisation's profits to charity or establishing "greener" business practises. There are a few major areas of social responsibility that many organisations today are pursuing.
- CSR is influenced by culture, religion, family values and customs, and industrialization.
- CSR enables both large and small enterprises to have a beneficial impact. It occurs when businesses make the decision to do the right thing not only for their profit line, but also to create consumer trust.

Businesses need energy to conduct their operations and provide services. Programs that focus on efficient power usage in buildings, such as heating, cooling, and lighting, as well as efficient fuel use and dependence on alternative fuel supplies, may reduce the demand for electricity in buildings. Clean water is regarded as a worldwide resource. Obtaining safe drinking water is seen as a basic human necessity, and it is included as one of a person's main rights. The provision of clean drinking water and health services for all people is one of the new millennium's development goals. Effective water management entails allocating water and managing its flow in order to accomplish just and long-term conservation of water resources. CSR is an important part of every business's operations.

"Corporate Social Responsibility is a hard-edged business decision. Not because it is a nice thing to do or because people are forcing us to do it because it is good for our business" -Niall Fitzerald, Former CEO, Unilever

There are two sorts of corporate social responsibility to take into account. The first entails businesses contributing money and resources to worthy social causes, such as donating money or employees time to organisations. This is the definition that many people think of when they think of corporate responsibility. Another sort of CSR, on the other hand, entails developing a concrete strategy to manufacture items or deliver services that are beneficial to society. Use of safe materials in design and manufacture, corporate environmental initiatives, and other reasons such as job creation and economic growth are all examples of these. The following areas may be recommended to meet some of these goals:

- Reducing gas emissions and waste, recycling resources, and replanting projects are all examples of environmental protection.
- Donating to charity and engaging in social causes, such as raising awareness about human rights and contemporary issues, are examples of charitable actions.

- Urban area development, in collaboration with the government, aims at reviving small businesses and improving the environment in smaller communities.
- Investment in local businesses, in collaboration with non-governmental organisations, in the areas of poverty reduction and social development initiatives.
- Projects that benefit employees, such as establishing greater standards for professional health and safety, providing equitable employment opportunities, and providing flexible work hours.
- Enterprise activities, operations, and services result in both direct and indirect emissions into the atmosphere. These emissions are caused by the company's goods, as well as its shopping habits and power use.
- Various pollutants, such as lead, mercury, volatile organic compounds, sulphur dioxide, nitric oxide, and other elements, may be released, resulting in environmental degradation and adverse impacts on human health. Those businesses whose operations generate liquid and solid waste should rely on waste reduction strategies. Reduced sources, reutilisation, recycling, waste treatment, and disposal must all be part of these initiatives.

To demonstrate a meaningful commitment to a cause, the most successful corporate social responsibility initiatives combine these two forms of CSR. An organisation that uses sustainable materials in its products, donates financial resources to environmental causes, and allows employees to volunteer at environmental charities on paid time off, for example, is demonstrating a true commitment to the environment that goes beyond any single CSR initiative. The relevance and popularity of social media is one of the reasons why organisations should have visible CSR programs.

Organisations that wish to safeguard their brand are aware that public opinion is influenced by social media.Whenan organisation engages in social responsibility through fundraising or employee giving programs, using social media to publicise these efforts helps to build a positive brand image, and it's a terrific opportunity to connect with your audience on a deeper level that goes beyond your products or services.

"We cannot lose sight of the fundamental challenges facing future generations. It's critical we take urgent action now to care for the planet and future generations. Asan organisation who looks to children as our role models, we are inspired by the millions of kids who have called for more urgent action on climate change." - Niels B Christiansen, LEGO Group CEO

Corporate social responsibility aims to enhance communities, the economy, and the environment. CSR, is a type of self-regulation that representsan organisation's accountability and commitment to contributing to the well-being of communities and society through a variety of environmental and social factors. CSR is critical to an organisation's brand impression, consumer, employee, and investor attraction, talent retention, and overall business success. Environmental initiatives, charitable work, ethical labour practises, and volunteer programs are all examples of CSR activities thatan organisation might employ.

"Profitability, growth rate, and brand recognition aren't the only factors that determine an organisation's success."

Customers, workers, and other stakeholders in today's world evaluatean organisation based on how its operations affect the community, economy, environment, and society as a whole. In other words, if it is concerned with the greater good rather than just the bottom line, corporate social responsibility practises are a means for your company to show its position on the issue. Corporate social responsibility (CSR) is a sort of self-regulation practised by businesses with the goal of social accountability and a positive influence on society.

Being environmentally responsible and eco-conscious; fostering equality, diversity, and inclusion in the workplace; treating workers with respect; giving back to the community; and ensuring business decisions are made with CSR in mind are just a few examples of how an organisation may embrace CSR:

- The environment is a major focus of corporate social responsibility. Businesses of all sizes have a significant carbon impact. Any efforts businesses may make to lower their carbon footprints are seen as beneficial to the firm as well as society as a whole. Businesses can also demonstrate social responsibility by giving to national and local charities.
- Businesses have a wealth of resources that may be used to support charities and community activities in their communities. Labor practises that are ethical Companies may show their corporate social responsibility by treating employees fairly and ethically. This is especially true for companies that operate in countries whose labour rules differ from those in the United States.

CSR has progressed from voluntary corporate decisions to required requirements at the regional, national, and international levels. Many businesses, on the other hand, prefer to go beyond their legal obligations and incorporate the concept of "doing good" into their business operations. There is no one-size-fits-all approach to CSR, but one thing is certain: foran organisation's policies to be viewed as authentic, they must be interwoven into its culture and business processes.

In today's socially conscious climate, employees and consumers value working for and spending money on companies that promote CSR. They have the ability to recognise corporate hypocrisy. The company fulfil the demands of customers, suppliers, shareholders, and workers, as well as the government, the general public, and the communities in which the company works, without jeopardising future generations' capacity to meet their own needs.an organisation's willingness to participate in volunteer events reveals a lot about its genuineness.

Organisations may demonstrate their concern for certain causes and support for specific groups by taking good actions without expecting anything in return. The CSR approach is comprehensive and integrated with the core business strategy for addressing social and environmental consequences of enterprises, as evidenced by the preceding criteria.

CSR must include the well-being of all stakeholders, not only the company's shareholders. CSR is made up of a much bigger collection of operations that have strategic commercial benefits in addition to philanthropic initiatives.

A company's values, business mission, and key concerns should all be examined to identify which activities best connect with the company's aims and culture. The company can either undertake the evaluation internally or pay a third party to do so. While general goals such as good health and well-being or gender equality may be applied to almost any business, specialised goals such as life below water or affordable and clean energy may be applicable to certain industries such as water technology or energy suppliers.Companies who have been doing CSR for a long time, with or without the law, only needed to simplify their spending. The issue or necessity for these companies wasn't so much about boosting spending by a factor of ten, but rather about having the opportunity to examine and re-strategise what they were currently doing in order to comply with the law's requirements. In addition to the retrofitting, a formal committee comprising a voluntary working group was formed.

Corporate social responsibility comes in a variety of shapes and sizes. A modest gift to a local food bank may have a big influence on social change, even for the tiniest businesses. The following are some of the most popular examples and checklist of CSR:

Examples:

- Carbon footprint reduction.
- Labor policies that are more favourable.
- Fairtrade participation.
- Inclusion, diversity, and equity.
- Philanthropic giving worldwide.
- Volunteering in the community and online.
- Environmentally friendly corporate policies.
- Investments that are both socially and ecologically aware.

Checklist:

- Provide a safer working environment and educational resources to employees?

- Would you like to improve your contractual relationships with your employees?
- Is it possible to use more energy-efficient appliances or vehicles?
- Are you sourcing more from local vendors? Is it possible to raise customer service standards?
- Would you want to contribute to more local community projects?
- Do you buy fair-trade items to help workers?
- Is it possible to recycle more waste?
- Make yourself more accessible to customers of varying abilities?

Companies that fall under the following categories are required to participate in CSR under the Companies Act of 2013: Companies with a net worth of at least Rs. 500 crore, a turnover of at least Rs. 1,000 crore, or a net profit of at least Rs. 5 crore are eligible.Among the organisational researchers who have attempted to identify and describe the various forms of CSR from time to time, the "Four-Part Model of Corporate Social Responsibility," proposed by Archie Carroll and later refined by Carroll and Buchholtz, is probably the most established and accepted model of CSR that addresses the forms of CSR.

A company's economic obligations include providing a reasonable return to investors, fair remuneration to employees, and goods at reasonable pricing to customers, among other things. As a result, achieving economic responsibility is the initial layer of accountability as well as the foundation for further accountability. The reality is that all organisations must fulfil economic responsibilities in order to thrive in the current era.

Legal implications businesses must follow the law of the nation and play by the rules of the game because of their legal responsibilities. Laws are the codification of society's dos and don'ts. Any organisation that wants to be socially responsible must follow the law. There have been several occasions in corporate history where laws have been broken and organisations were no longer able to operate. Enron, Union Carbide, Global Trust Bank, and other instructive corporate incidents of societal rejection and boycott include, for example, Enron, Union Carbide, and Global Trust Bank.

Moral Responsibilities pertain to corporate commitments that are correct, equitable, and fair. Following the law, process, and rules and regulations does not always imply that corporate activity is ethical or beneficial. Corporate behaviour that goes beyond the law and contributes to societal well-being is said to be ethical. As a result, companies have an ethical obligation to do what is beneficial to society, even if it goes beyond the rules and regulations. To put it another way, ethical duties are what society expects from companies in addition to their economic and legal obligations.

The Greek term philanthropy literally means "love of one's neighbour." The application of this concept in the business world includes efforts that are, of course, within the corporation's discretion to improve the quality of life of workers, local communities, and, ultimately, society. Corporate Social Responsibility (CSR) has been practised in India for decades. CSR has been a popular topic in recent years as a result of such illustrious instances. Indian CSR is on the rise. The accessibility and efficacy of CSR initiatives are further hampered by a lack of awareness, insufficiently educated employees, coverage, policy, and other factors.

A large number of businesses are engaging in these activities on the surface and marketing them in the media. Public relations is an effective strategy for influencing customer perceptions and enhancingan organisation's image. Corporations that actively promote their social responsibility efforts frequently use the media to highlight their work. Publicising business donations, employees volunteer programs, and other CSR activities is a strong branding strategy that may help you gain exposure in both online and print media.

When it comes to working with politicians and government authorities, companies that prioritise corporate social responsibility usually have an easier time. Businesses that show a reckless disdain for social responsibility, on the other hand, frequently find themselves defending themselves against numerous inquiries and probes, which are frequently initiated at the request of public service groups.

The more positive public opinion is, the better. The less likely activist organisations are to initiate public campaigns and seek government investigations againstan organisation with good public opinion that it takes social responsibility seriously. Finally, one of the most significant advantages of fostering social responsibility at work is the good atmosphere you create for your colleagues.

Employees and management will be more excited and involved in their tasks if they believe they work foran organisation with a real conscience. This may foster a sense of belonging and collaboration, bringing everyone together and resulting in happier, more productive workers. The fundamental problem for organisations that perceive CSR as a way to grow their company is implementation. A viable path forward can be found through smart cooperation.

What exactly is Strategic Corporate Social Responsibility (SCSR)?

Organisations may evaluate what actions they have the resources to spend on being socially responsible and choose those that will increase their competitive advantage by taking a strategic approach. Organisations may guarantee that earnings and increasing shareholder value do not eclipse the requirement to behave ethically toward their stakeholders by including CSR into their entire strategy.

Strategic CSR provides organisations with solutions for balancing the creation of economic value with the creation of societal value; recognising and responding to threats and opportunities that their stakeholders face; and evaluating the organisation's capacity for charitable endeavours and sustainable business methods. CSR in business is the driving force behind all you do. Profit-seeking businesses also contribute to some areas of societal development, but clearly not all. It is unrealistic to expect every corporation to be active in every facet of social development. The expenses of implementing CSR will be higher, but the benefits will almost certainly surpass the expenditures. The terrible events of September 11th have given global issues a new dimension. The fall of Enron and WorldCom, as well as its auditor, Arthur Andersen, as a result of questionable accounting methods, has increased scrutiny of huge corporations and their auditors.

Companies are becoming increasingly aware of the need to project a socially conscious image. When it comes to picking a brand or firm, consumers, workers, and stakeholders value CSR, and they hold corporations accountable for affecting social change via their principles, policies, and profits. To stand out from the crowd, your business must demonstrate to the public that it is a force for good. Advocating for and raising awareness for socially significant topics is a great approach for your company to stay top-of-mind and boost brand value.

According to the Kantar Purpose 2020 study, there is a direct link between perceived positive effect and increased brand value. Over the course of 12 years, companies having a high positive effect grew their brand value by 175%, whereas organisations with a low positive impact grew by just 70%. Schmidt also stated that sustainable development might be beneficial toan organisation's bottom line. Reduced manufacturing costs can be achieved by using less packaging and less energy, for example.

If you demonstrate a well-developed CSR program and efforts, your firm will become more desirable to existing and potential investors. Investors are becoming more important stakeholders in corporate social responsibility, according to CECP's authoritative 2021 Giving in Numbers report. Almost 80% of the organisations polled said they were willing to share data and examine their viewpoints on sustainability. When it comes to social responsibility, investors, like customers, are holding organisations accountable. At the same time, an organisation that takes CSR seriously sends a message to both investors and partners that it cares about both long-term and short-term success.

What are the rewarding effects of CSR?

Innovation By applying the "lens of sustainability," as McDonald put it, Unilever was able to develop new goods such as a water-saving hair conditioner. The company's research and development efforts may not have resulted in such a product if it hadn't been for sustainability. Cost-cutting One of the simplest ways for a corporation to become involved in sustainability is to use it as a cost-cutting tool. General Mills, for example, has set a goal of reducing energy consumption by 20% by 2015.

Brand differentiation (for example, Timberland), for example, was able to develop their voice and implement their principles into their business strategy. Customer participation What good is corporate social responsibility if no one knows about it? Wal-Mart has positioned itself as a leader in environmental measures in recent years. This is an underutilised instrument for company-to-company communication.

Motivating employees, for example, Sara Lee established a cross-functional, worldwide Sustainability Working Team to assist in the development of a sustainability strategy. The Solo Cup Company launched the Sustainability Action Network to engage workers in community service centred on the company's CSR initiatives at a more grassroots level.

Keeping social responsibility at the forefront of one's thoughts helps organisations act ethically and examine their company's social and environmental consequences. Giving employees the option to participate in an organisation's socially responsible initiatives can benefit employees by teaching them new skills that they can apply in the workplace. By engaging in activities outside of their normal job obligations, employees can contribute to projects and issues that they are passionate about or learn something completely new that will assist in improving their own views.

Organisations stimulate growth and development by sponsoring these activities. Organisations enhance employee growth and support by sponsoring these activities. Increased productivity and quality; improved capacity to recruit and retain employees; reduced regulatory scrutiny; improved access to financing; diversification of the workforce; product safety and liability reduction; contributions to charity; employee volunteer programs; corporate engagement in community education, employment, and homelessness initiatives; product safety and quality; social advantages: as increased use of renewable resources; integration of environmental management tools into company planning, including life-cycle assessment and costing; assessment and costing, environmental management standards, and eco-labeling. It may help existing and prospective clients strengthen links, form alliances, and develop solid business partnerships. As a result, it is possible to achieve public-value results that would not have been possible otherwise.

Differentiation of brands CSR can aid in the development of client loyalty based on shared ethical ideals. Some businesses use their commitment to CSR as a major selling point. Some businesses utilise CSR approaches as a strategic tool to acquire public support for their worldwide presence, allowing them to maintain a competitive edge by exploiting their social contributions as another type of advertising. For example, when Dettol developed its cause-related marketing strategy, in which a shilling is contributed to charity for every product purchased, Dettol goods gained appeal in the marketplace, separating themselves from other antibacterial products.

Long before the term became widespread, companies like Tata and Birla in India have been practising Corporate Social Responsibility (CSR) for decades. Despite having such illustrious precedents, CSR in India is still in its early stages. CSR programs' reach and efficacy are further hampered by a lack of awareness, insufficiently educated people, coverage, policy, and other factors. A large number of organisations are engaging in these actions on the surface and promoting and highlighting them in the media. This study paper investigates and evaluates the concerns and obstacles that CSR operations in India confront. Corporate social responsibility has been firmly entrenched in the global business agenda.

However, numerous obstacles must be overcome in order to transition from theory to practice. Corporate social responsibility has been firmly entrenched in the global business agenda. However, several difficulties must be overcome in order to get from theory to action. The need for more accurate measures of progress in the field of CSR, as well as the distribution of CSR plans, is a major problem for businesses. Transparency and discussion may helpan organisation look more trustworthy while also raising the standards of other businesses. The following are some of the beneficial consequences that can occur when corporations implement a social responsibility policy:The requirements include spending at least 2% of profits on CSR and establishing a dedicated committee on their board to oversee execution.

As a result of this law, India is the only country in the world with a CSR law. In order to comply with the rules of the Enterprises Act, 2013, about 8,500 Indian companies would be obliged to execute CSR initiatives under this new legislation. Many businesses will be taking these steps for the first time. According to estimates, corporate social responsibility commitments might total up to Rs. 20,000 crore every year. CSR has been practised by Indian businesses for decades.

Many major corporations, such as Tata, Wipro, and Maruti, have successfully implemented their programs. However, the vast majority of them are still useless. Lack of awareness of the industry and challenges, target recipients, insufficiently trained people, coverage, and other factors all contribute to CSR's ineffectiveness. Some businesses engage in these actions ostensibly for the purpose of promoting them in the media. Major CSR projects are undertaken by Indian corporations. CSR has always been viewed as a charity activity in India.

As a result, documentation on particular operations linked to this notion is scarce. However, it was apparent that much of this had a national flavour to it, whether it was endowing institutions or actively engaging in India's liberation fight, and it was encompassed in the concept of trusteeship.

The strength of customer pressure knows no bounds. Consumer concerns are taken into account by even major conventional enterprises. For example, Lego has set a goal of using only renewable energy to power its manufacturing facilities. The Danish corporation was able to achieve this target even sooner than expected because of the installation of an offshore wind farm. Wind farm Lego kits are currently available. One step companies are taking to boost this sort of consumer reaction is by working to be a "millennial-friendly"organisation to create trust with community members. An organisation that is prepared to produce or support socially responsible projects demonstrates to customers that they have the value alignment that their target audience seeks, whether it be through waste reduction, charitable giving, or encouraging opportunities in their community.

As several commentators have noted, CSR in India is still mostly philanthropic, but it has shifted from institutional construction (educational, scientific, and cultural) to community development through various initiatives. Furthermore, as global influences and communities become more active and demanding, there appears to be a discernible trend that, while CSR remains largely limited to community development, it is becoming more strategic in nature (i.e., becoming linked to business) than philanthropic, and a large number of companies are reporting their activities in this space on their official websites, annual reports, sustainability reports, and even publishing books.

If an organisation does not explore waste reduction, clean water efforts, or other environmentally friendly solutions, it will be missing out on a significant market of customers who want to buy from companies that are socially responsible and sustainable, as well as companies that share their values. This is a setback.

When it comes to developing a socially responsible company strategy, there are a few things to avoid. It is possible to become a socially responsible business with a few restrictions.

- Avoid volunteering for charitable causes that are unrelated to your primary business or that in any way contradict your company's ethical standards.
- Instead of giving money to a completely unrelated group, find a nonprofit that your organisation believes in or invest in a project in your neighbourhood.
- Don't use CSR opportunities only to promote your company.

According to Schmidt, running a corporate responsibility campaign as a fast marketing strategy might backfire if your company doesn't follow through. Rather than attempting a one-time stunt, gradually implement socially acceptable corporate practises.

According to Schmidt, employees and customers respond favourably to businesses that prioritise long-term social responsibility. Don't wait for the rest of the industry to catch up to you. Don't delay if you're thinking of sustainable actions that aren't yet legally obligatory. You may set the benchmark for your industry and enhance your process by embracing socially responsible rules early on. Taking part in CSR projects benefits everyone involved. Your actions will not only appeal to socially conscious customers and employees, but they will also have a real world impact.

Adidas is fighting plastic pollution by collaborating with Parley to transform garbage into high-performance gear. They've also staged Run For The Oceans events to raise cash since 2018. They're also collaborating with Greenpeace on the DETOX Campaign, which aims to remove hazardous chemicals from global supply chains. This entailed collaborating with other brands in order to meet the campaign's objectives. Starbucks is a supporter of Ethos Water, a global effort that aspires to provide clean water to 1 billion people.

The Ethos Water Fund is run by the Starbucks Foundation, and proceeds from the sale of Ethos Water bottles go to support the program. For more than two decades, the Starbucks Foundation has supported local communities in both the United States and throughout the world. For more than two decades, the Starbucks Foundation has been investing in local communities in the United States and across the world. This includes a major focus on groups that assist people in overcoming hurdles to employment and training. Tamana, Grow Trees, KK Academy, and the World Monument Fund are among the organisations with whom IndiGoReach has collaborated.

Children, education, female empowerment, the environment, and heritage are all important aspects of their social responsibilities. Uptill now, their collaborations have assisted in the empowerment of over 64,000 women, the education of over 47,000 children, and the planting of over 40,000 trees. IKEA's commitment to social responsibility begins with the materials they use in their goods, which include organic cotton, wool, and wood. By 2030, they intend to use exclusively recycled or renewable plastic. They help more households transcend poverty by establishing a sustainable income through the IKEA Foundation.

Climate action, renewable energy, agricultural livelihoods, employment and entrepreneurship, and disaster response are among the programs they support. They collaborate with NGOs and other partners to implement these initiatives. Bosch is committed to investing in programs that assist communities across the world to solve difficulties. To accomplish this, they collaborate with a number of organisations, including the New Sunshine Charity Foundation. Since 2018, Apple has been a Laureate partner with the Malala Fund to help educate and empower girls. Since 2014, they've been members of the ConnectED project, which sponsors teaching and learning solutions in schools across the United States.

Coca-Cola distributes at least 1% of its yearly operating profits to charitable organisations and causes. They've been assisting Arwa's "Price of Water" initiative in providing safe drinking water to refugees in the Middle East since 2014. BMW collaborates with groups to achieve their CSR objectives of encouraging diversity, motivating the next generation of engineers, supporting social mobility and inclusion, and educating people about road safety. They also urge their employees to contribute to causes and organisations that they care about.

Dell aims to utilise its technology and experience to help the world change for the better. In 2019, their employees volunteered 5 million hours to local charities. This was mostly a skills-based situation. Their technology has been used to improve the Indian government's preventative healthcare system, give speedier treatments for critically ill children, and assist in educating more children throughout the world.

Microsoft provides CSR programs that focus on boosting skills and employability as well as environmental sustainability. Through Microsoft Philanthropies, they work with NGOs, organisations, and schools to advance computer science education and create greater impact through technology. They also support groups that work to enhance Washington residents' quality of life. Employee giving is a key element of Microsoft's corporate culture; therefore, workers also support initiatives in their local areas. They provide their time and skills to organisations in addition to donating money. Microsoft matches employee contributions both financially and in terms of time. If you're seeking CSR ideas for your company, here are some examples of large-scale CSR initiatives:

LEGO has invested millions of dollars in addressing climate change and waste reduction.Reduced packaging, sustainable materials, and investments in alternative energy are among LEGO's ecologically aware endeavours.

To promote physical and mental health as well as educational possibilities, TOMS distributes one-third of its net income to organisations. During the epidemic, all charity donations were routed to the TOMS COVID-19 Global Giving Fund.

The Johnson & Johnson brand invests in alternative energy sources to reduce its environmental impact. Johnson & Johnson also strives to provide communities with clean, safe water on a global scale. To diversify its employees, the multinational coffee company has adopted a socially responsible recruiting procedure. It is focusing its efforts on hiring more veterans, young people just starting out in their careers, and refugees. By investing in renewable energy sources and environmentally friendly offices,

Google has proved its dedication to the environment. Sundar Pichai, the company's CEO, is well known for taking a position on social concerns. Pfizer's commitment to corporate responsibility is evident in its healthcare activities, which include raising awareness about non-infectious illnesses and providing affordable health care to women and children in developing countries.

These businesses are taking significant steps to better their communities and the globe in general. These 10 projects set the standard for this year's most creative enterprises in the field of corporate social responsibility, from sustainably made shoes to mitigating 75 years of carbon waste. Most innovative Companies in the field of corporate social responsibility in 2021 are:

1. Microsoft:

Setting extremely lofty long-term carbon-neutrality targets. Not only is Microsoft vowing to become carbon neutral by 2030, but also to erase all of the carbon the firm has ever released since its creation in 1975 by 2050, going above and beyond most conventional corporate climate promises. It plans to do so by establishing a climate-related innovation fund, growing its internal carbon charge, and assisting suppliers and customers in reducing their carbon footprints. And, in order to reach zero waste by 2030, it has made the daring promise of diverting at least 90% of its landfill trash and making all Surface devices totally recyclable.

2. Grove Collaborative:

For pledging to eliminate all plastic from its products. It plans to do so by establishing a climate-related innovation fund, growing its internal carbon charge, and assisting suppliers and customers in reducing their carbon footprints. And, in order to reach zero waste by 2030, it has made the daring promise of diverting at least 90% of its landfill trash and making all Surface devices totally recyclable.This natural goods shop aspires to be completely plastic-free by 2025. In 2020, it took a step toward that aim by developing a 100% plastic-free range of household cleaning goods that instead use glass and aluminium containers. It also introduced Peach, a new personal care line of waterless, plastic-free, plant-based products that the company hopes will save 70,000 pounds of plastic in less than a year of sales.

3. Capital One

Over the course of the summer, the company's Capital One Coders summer program grew by 400 percent, transitioning to a virtual classroom format to engage predominantly low-to-moderate-income children in technology through problem-solving methodologies. To teach about AI, it added an app creator and a bot camp to its extended curriculum. They also provided much-needed digital connectivity to 2,500 households at a time when many youngsters without access to Wi-Fi have struggled to attend virtual classes.

4. Logitech

That is unrivalled in the industry for its clarity on carbon emissions.The consumer electronics design firm has committed to "complete carbon transparency," pledging to mark all goods with a carbon footprint figure. By 2025, it hopes to have those numbers—along with universally accessible symbols—printed throughout its entire portfolio, allowing customers to make educated decisions and hold the company responsible.

5. Clio

During the epidemic, to increase access to free legal advice in collaboration with the American Bar Association, this Canadian legal cloud software business launched a pro-bono platform to link attorneys with those in need of legal assistance for concerns related to the epidemic, such as housing, unemployment benefits, and domestic abuse. Clio's main objective is to remove financial obstacles to legal representation, and this invention is part of that mission.

6. Verizon

For helping low-income youngsters connect at home and bridging the "homework gap." As the pandemic spread, Verizon Innovative Learning ramped up its efforts to provide under-resourced schoolchildren with their own built-in technology devices and free data plans, allowing them to comfortably engage in distance learning and overcome the "digital divide" that has left so many low-income children reliant on Wi-Fi from nearby buildings. They've also blended sophisticated technology into learning: in Miami, enrolled students functioned as IT troubleshooters for school systems transitioning to virtual learning, while others in Cleveland 3D-printed personal protective equipment for important employees.

7. Bitwise Industries

For using its technical expertise to offer food and resources to people. As the epidemic spread, this tech ecosystem pledged to combine its specialised knowledge to create digital initiatives that would help underprivileged people gain access to the necessities they so sorely needed. Its software engineers created an app to manage grocery orders and track food delivery, resulting in 200,000 meals being delivered across California's Central Valley. Separately, it launched a network that connected newly jobless individuals with employment and assistance, initially in California with Governor Newsom's support, and later across much of the United States.

Paternalistic philanthropy has a long history in India, do you agree?

CSR is an increasing trend among corporations, and it's also a wonderful method for NGOs to diversify their revenue and reach out to new supporters. Companies that are socially responsible are putting their resources to good use in their communities (both local and global). Many NGOs aren't realising the benefits of CSR collaborations, owing to a lack of knowledge about how to get started. Even if your business is tiny, you may still benefit from bringing in CSR partners and using their cash, resources, and support to promote your cause.

By caring about problems like Earth Day, raising awareness, and encouraging social change, corporate social responsibility helps build customer trust. Thousands of organisations are contributing, but the activities of huge multinational corporations have far-reaching consequences that can affect global concerns such as hunger and health, as well as global warming and climate change.

At the initial stage charity and philanthropy were the primary motivations for CSR in the early stages. Wealthy merchants shared a portion of their riches with the wider society during the pre-industrialisation period, which lasted until 1850, by erecting temples for religious purposes. Industrial dynasties such as Tata, Godrej, Bajaj, Modi, Birla, and Singhania were highly influenced by economic and social issues in the nineteenth century.

However, it has been recognised that their efforts toward social and industrial progress were affected by caste groupings and political interests in addition to unselfish and religious objectives. During the second phase of the independence struggle, there was a greater emphasis on Indian industrialists' demonstrating their commitment to the advancement of society. This was the time when Mahatma Gandhi created the concept of "trusteeship," which required business executives to manage their riches in order to help the common man. The Final Stage The third phase of CSR (1960–80) was linked to the "mixed economy" feature, the creation of public sector undertakings (PSUs), and labour and environmental legislation. The Final Stage Indian corporations began abandoning their conventional CSR participation in the fourth phase (1980–2013) and integrating it into a long-term business plan. CSR in India is undergoing a transformation.

The Corporate Social Responsibility (CSR) law went into force on April 1, 2014, and it's been a little over a year since then. The entire landscape of CSR in India has undergone a drastic turn in such a short time. Companies that are qualified under section 135 of the Companies Act 2013 have embraced the law and launched a slew of CSR initiatives across the board, as stated in Schedule VII of the Act.

CSR encompasses not only the development activities thatan organisation performs but also the processes that a corporation uses to make responsible investments and provide transparency to diverse stakeholders, among other things. Recognising the value of socially responsible business practises, they have implemented them. CSR's main goal is to optimisean organisation's total influence on society and stakeholders while also addressing the environment and long-term viability.

CSR encompasses not only the development activities that an organisation performs but also the techniques thatan organisation is responsible for. Despite its newfound popularity, the method has been used since ancient times, although unofficially. Philosophers from India, such as Kautilya, and philosophers from the pre-Christian era in the West, advocated and encouraged ethical ideals in business. Several ancient texts mention the principle of assisting the poor and disadvantaged. Philanthropy, religion, and charity were the primary drivers of CSR prior to the industrial revolution. Charity and other social issues were important to industrial households in the nineteenth century.

However, the payments, whether monetary or non-monetary, were occasional acts of charity or philanthropy made from personal funds that did not belong to the shareholders and did not form part of the business. The industrial families also built temples, schools, higher education institutions, and other public facilities during this time. In the early 1970s, the term "corporate social responsibility" became popular. The last ten years of the twentieth century saw a change in emphasis away from charity and conventional philanthropy and toward more direct commercial participation in mainstream development and concern for underprivileged sections of society. There is a growing recognition in India that business cannot flourish in isolation and that social change is required for long-term success.

In India, where there is a huge divide between parts of the population in terms of income and standards, as well as socio-economic position, an ideal CSR approach incorporates both ethical and philosophical components.CSR has expanded fast in India over the last decade, with some corporations concentrating on strategic CSR activities to help improve the country.

Companies in India gradually began to focus on need-based programs that coincided with national goals, including public health, education, livelihoods, water conservation, and natural resource management. In the last 10 years, there have been extensive national discussions about the business sector's possible role and duty in addressing social challenges.In its emphasis on getting businesses to join in solving social and developmental challenges as part of their social responsibility and business operations, The Department of Public Enterprises released standards for spending on CSR initiatives for central public sector enterprises, setting an example for the private sector.

In 2021, the Sustainable Development Goals (SDGs) will be included in the responsible business actions of 80% of the top 100 organisations for sustainability and CSR. CSR had an especially bad year in the year 2021. In comparison to the previous year, CSR expenditure in the country declined by 64% in FY 2020–21. CSR spending in the past financial year amounted to Rs. 8,828.11 crore, according to official statistics given to the federal legislative body, a significant decrease from Rs. 24,688.66 crore in FY

2019–20 and Rs. 20,150.27 crore in FY 2018–19.

Godrej Consumer Goods has topped the CSR rating list for the first time in 2021, followed by Infosys and Wipro, which have been continuous star performers. In addition, two Tata enterprises rank among the top ten. In FY 2021, IT was the best-performing industry in terms of CSR. Godrej Consumer Products Limited isan organisation that manufactures consumer goods. In the fiscal year 2020–21, Godrej Consumer Products Ltd. (GCPL) spent Rs. 34.08 crore on CSR projects. Over 2.77 lakh people from the most vulnerable groups were addressed by the company's CSR programs. GCPL redirected 63% of their CSR funding to start medium-to long-term livelihood recovery programs for over 9000 nano entrepreneurs during the previous fiscal year. The majority of its CSR projects have been carried out through the Infosys Foundation, which was founded in 1996, long before the nation's CSR mandate was lifted. The firm spent Rs. 325.32 crores on CSR projects in FY 2020–21.

Wipro's CSR initiatives are carried out through a variety of channels, the most prominent of which being the Wipro Foundation. In the previous financial year, the firm spent Rs. 251 crores on CSR. Wipro has sponsored over 1,561 initiatives spanning humanitarian relief, integrated healthcare, and livelihood regeneration in the previous 12 months, with a total impact of over 10 million people as a result of its COVID-19 response. As a result, over 10.2 million people have received food, dry rations, and personal hygiene kits. As a result, 330 million meals have been distributed, over 8.2 million people have had their livelihoods restored, and more than 500 non-profits involved in humanitarian and healthcare aid have been supported. Through mohalla lessons, distribution of worksheets, books, and other materials, the company's education efforts were helpful in reaching over 1.1 lakh pupils throughout 14 states.

Tata Chemicals has been one of the most prominent sustainability champions in recent years. The organisation has undertaken a number of environmental initiatives and projects, as well as working with local communities to create a sustainable and environmentally friendly environment. In FY21, the company spent Rs. 21 crore on CSR initiatives. In the previous financial year, the firm helped 6,878 farmers with capacity building, field demonstrations, and livestock management through digital and physical contacts. It also supported Okhai's rural women artisans, transforming the region into a bazaar with 25,190 participants. Through mohalla lessons, distribution of worksheets, books, and other materials, the company's education efforts were helpful in reaching over 1.1 lakh pupils throughout 14 states. At Mithapur, the corporation has planted 1.15 lakh mangroves across several areas as part of its greening effort, which also includes the protection of native plant species.

The concept that an organisation must serve a greater societal purpose while keeping national interests in mind drives ITC's sustainability activities. The company's mission to concurrently develop economic, social, and environmental capital, known as the Triple Bottom Line, has choreographed a symphony of attempts to solve some of the most difficult societal concerns, such as pervasive poverty and environmental degradation. The company's social forestry initiative greened 30,439 acres of land in the previous fiscal year.

Through its education initiative, the corporation was able to reach 0.33 million youngsters. During the year, it supplied skills to 12,470 young people through vocational training programs. In 28 areas, it helped fund the building of 640 individual family toilets. Jubilant Life Sciences Limited was ranked in the top ten corporations for CSR this year, up from 23rd the previous year. The Jubilant Bhartia Foundation is in charge of the majority of Jubilant Life Sciences' CSR projects. Through several social development programs in the realms of health, education, livelihood, and social entrepreneurship, the company's CSR actions are reaching out to nearly 6.5 million people in 240 communities. Grasim Industries Limited has increased its CSR spending by nearly 45 percent since the previous fiscal year.In FY 2020–21, it spent Rs. 84.66 crores, up from Rs. 47.14 crores in FY20.

The Economic Times and Futurescape Responsible Business Rankings 2020 named it 9th among India's Top Companies for Sustainability and CSR. This year, it has risen to 7th place on the list. Grasim's social outreach network spans 15 places in India, encompassing seven states. Through its CSR initiatives, the firm was able to affect the lives of nearly 31.6 lakh individuals in FY21. Since the previous fiscal year, Grasim Industries Limited has increased its CSR spending by nearly 45 percent.In FY 2020–21, it spent Rs. 84.66 crores, up from Rs. 47.14 crores in FY20.

The Economic Times and Futurescape Responsible Business Rankings 2020 named it 9th among India's Top Companies for Sustainability and CSR. Last year, it had risen to 7th place on the list. Grasim's social outreach network spans 15 places in India, encompassing seven states. Through its CSR initiatives, the firm was able to affect the lives of nearly 31.6 lakh individuals in FY21. Vedanta Limited is involved in a variety of CSR efforts, including water, energy, and carbon management. Across our core impact areas of education, health, sustainable livelihoods, women's empowerment, sports and culture, environment, and community development, Vedanta spent approximately Rs. 331 crore on social development programs in FY2021.

Tata Power has climbed to number 10 in the CSR rankings, up from 57th the previous year. In 2020-21, the electric utility firm spent Rs. 3.45 crore on CSR. Financial inclusion, education, health and sanitation, water, livelihoods and skill building are the five main areas of its CSR projects.

JSW Steel Limited believes that superior goods, sustained growth, and CSR activities create value for all of its stakeholders. In the fiscal year 2020–21, the firm spent Rs. 78.32 crores on CSR, with an extra Rs. 86.49 crores put into the unspent CSR account. UPL is a global agricultural goods and solutions company. In India, the corporation paid Rs. 100 crore for CSR, with Rs. 75 crore going to the PM CARES Fund to combat the epidemic. The CSR team undertook multiple activities around the country in 2020–21 to satisfy the development requirements of various communities. As part of Project Pace in Pratapgarh and Sultanpur, UPL is assisting the TYCIA Foundation in delivering better education. UPL will finance the education of 100 kids as part of this effort, which will also include the creation of basic infrastructure. The business has built 120 solar lights in Rajasthan's Barmer and 95 solar lights in Madhya Pradesh's Singhbara and Morena.

During the fiscal years 2020–21, Mahindra & Mahindra Ltd. invested Rs. 92.78 crore in different CSR initiatives across India. This figure excludes the company's Rs. 20 crore commitment to the PM CARES Fund in FY 2020. M &

M Ltd. isan organisation based in the United Kingdom. Dr. Reddy's Laboratories is a Hyderabad-based international pharmaceutical company. This year, it spent more on corporate social responsibility than was required. The pharma business spent Rs. 36.08 crores on CSR in FY2021, instead of the mandated Rs. 34.1 crores. During the three years prior to the current financial year, Tech Mahindra spent more than 2% of its average net income on CSR. The corporation made a major contribution to COVID-19 relief efforts this year. A total of Rs. 105 crore was spent on corporate social responsibility programs.

The TMF team altered its focus as soon as the COVID-19 epidemic broke out, to provide help to those who were the worst impacted—daily wagers, migrant workers, farmers, people with disabilities, and the transgender community. The Foundation supplied over 6 lakh ration packages, 3.20 lakh prepared meals, PPE kits, masks, and medical equipment to hospitals through systematic and effective action. Over the course of the year, relief activities of Rs. 14.82 crores were carried out, with work continuing into the current financial year. Over 20 million individuals have benefited from these initiatives to date.

In addition to the government's efforts to combat COVID-19, Hindustan Unilever was one of the first companies to pledge Rs. 100 crores to societal activity. In FY2021, the corporation spent Rs. 165.08 crores on corporate social responsibility. In partnership with the government and various NGOs, HUL donated over 2 crore soaps and sanitisers, bottles of toilet and surface cleaners, Horlicks packs, and other products to frontline medical professionals, police officers, sanitation workers, and vulnerable citizens of the country in a partnership with the government and various NGOs during the pandemic.

Ambuja Cement is a significant participant in the Indian cement market and is known for its custom-made product line that is appropriate for a variety of climatic situations in India.

In FY2021, Rs. 53.97 crores were spent on CSR initiatives, significantly more than the mandated amount. Toyota Kirloskar Motor (TKM) is a joint venture between Toyota Motor Corporation Japan and Kirloskar Systems Limited that was founded in India in 1997. Toyota's position in the global automotive environment serves as motivation for TKM. By promoting active local engagement, the firm thinks it can create localised solutions that are sustainable. In this context, the CSR team has designed and constructed a sustainable community development model, in which basic community interventions at the local level are made.In this context, the CSR team has designed and constructed a long-term community development model in which basic community interventions are refined over time into more strategic and comprehensive collaborations.

Long before the Companies Act of 2013 compelled CSR, L&T was providing health and educational services to the needy in the communities surrounding its campuses. L&T's CSR programs are well-established now, concentrating on sectors that match with global and national development objectives, such as water and sanitation, health, education, and skill development. In FY 2020-21, total CSR spending was Rs. 150.06 crores, or 2.062 percent of earnings after tax, which is higher than the minimum 2%.

L&T's CSR has been on the frontlines in a variety of ways, including establishing ICUs for treating COVID-19 patients, equipping government hospitals with ventilators, providing Personal Protective Equipment (PPE) kits, gloves, and masks to health workers, and making basic provisions such as food available to those in need. The majority of the CSR program employees accepted responsibility for educating communities in the project areas about preventative and safety measures, and they were accessible for counselling and referrals.

NTPC Limited, India's largest power company, is a statutory Indian business. In the fiscal year 2020–21, it spent Rs. 418.87 crore on CSR projects, exceeding the mandated 2 percent amount of Rs. 278.57 crore and achieving a CSR expenditure of 3.04 percent.The corporation donated Rs. 250 crores to the PM CARES Fund to aid the government's fight against COVID-19. NTPC earned the FICCI Jury Commendation Certificate under the Category "Women Empowerment" for its flagship CSR project "Girl Empowerment Mission" at the CII-ITC Sustainability Award-2020 for "Corporate Social Responsibility" (GEM).

Hindustan Zinc is the world's sixth largest silver producer and India's sole integrated silver, lead, and zinc producer. HZL is a subsidiary of Vedanta Limited, which owns 64.9 percent of the firm, while the Indian government holds 29.5 percent. In FY2021, HZL spent Rs. 214 crores on CSR. The "Integrated Health and Wellbeing Council" awarded Hindustan Zinc the CSR Health Effect Award in 2021 as a symbol of gratitude for its extraordinary reaction and on-the-ground activities with a strong focus on life, livelihood, and mitigating the impact of the COVID-19 epidemic.

Companies that are socially responsible use their power and resources for more than just gratifying their shareholders and expanding their profits. They use a business strategy that emphasises social impact and rewards their local and global communities for their achievements. This isn't to suggest that profit is unimportant to socially conscious businesses (probably not the most sustainable step for for-profit companies). No, businesses are simply accepting their duty to improve the well-being of the communities from which they profit and are weaving that responsibility into the fabric of their operations. Companies are increasingly incorporating corporate social responsibility (CSR) programs into their operations and associating themselves with social movements that are gaining traction.

CSR strategies vary with each company, but they often include charitable fundraising, working conditions, social benefits such as health care, volunteerism, and environmental stewardship. And other businesses go beyond a program to make social responsibility a part of their DNA. While it's unknown if organisations like JP Morgan and Amazon will act to meet their pledges to social justice and sustainability, the trend is clear: companies recognise that customers value the good of society over the good of the company's shareholders, and they're responding accordingly.

Why do newer generations want more corporate social responsibility?

Millennials want more corporate social responsibility. Socially responsible businesses are much more essential to millennials and Generation Z. They think that businesses should invest in improving society and seek out solutions that would help them do so. Companies should communicate how they are attempting to have a beneficial influence on the globe so that the general public may witness their pro-social efforts. It's critical to understand how to sell to millennials since your efforts will influence the decisions they make as customers.

Millennials also like to participate in activities such as volunteer work and philanthropy. As more businesses see the influence of their socially and environmentally conscious initiatives on consumer perception, the more likely it is that they will follow suit. As more organisations see the influence of their socially and ecologically conscious activities on customer perception, the more likely they are to launch their own projects.

As Millennials and Gen Z become the economy's driving force, appreciation for socially responsible corporate practises continues to grow. As a result of these two generations' purchasing perspectives, consumer attention has turned to social responsibility, particularly when it comes to the environment. According to a Nielsen survey conducted in 2018, 85% of Millennials and 80 percent of Gen Z regard the environment as the most important factor in deciding which companies to connect with.

CSR is a means for businesses to give back to the community and assist groups that share their values. Matching gift schemes, gifts of dollars or products, and volunteer grant programs are all examples of this. Many well-known companies have embraced CSR and joined with a variety of charitable organisations to effect change. With their CSR activities, many socially responsible businesses have a direct influence on society. Consumers believe that by purchasing a product or service from a socially responsible firm, they are helping to make the world a better place. The more socially responsiblean organisation is, the more its community and customers support it.

According to studies, consumers are increasingly prepared to spend extra when they know their purchases will have a positive impact. Consumer decision-making has been demonstrated to be influenced by environmental friendliness alone, with a rising percentage of customers throughout the world expressing interest in and readiness to pay for ecologically friendly items. Customers are active participants in the world-saving quest to prevent climate change, and they're eager to support the businesses that are fighting with them. The effect isn't entirely external. Employees are asking more and more if their job has a beneficial social impact. Employees are increasingly seeking social fulfilment from their hours spent on the job at a time when the barrier between work and personal life is becoming increasingly blurred. The list of world's top brands' CSR aspirations 2021 is given below:

Rank 1. Johnson & Johnson, Inc.
Rank 2. Google
Rank 3. Coca-Cola
Rank 4. Ford Motors
Rank 5. Netflix
Rank 6. Spotify
Rank 7. Pfizer
Rank 8. Wells Fargo
Rank 9. Toms
Rank 10. Bosch
Rank 11. General Electric
Rank 12. Starbucks
Rank 13. The Walt Disney
Rank 14. Lego

CSR has been the subject of several discussions and studies over the last few years. CSR is a type of self-regulation that representsan organisation's accountability and commitment to contributing to the well-being of communities and society. CSR aims to enhance communities, the economy, and the environment. Corporate social responsibility is a sort of self-regulation practised by businesses with the goal of social accountability and a positive influence on society.

Corporations that actively promote their social responsibility efforts frequently use the media to highlight their work. When it comes to developing a socially responsible company strategy, there are a few things to avoid. One of the most significant advantages of fostering social responsibility at work is the good atmosphere you create for your colleagues.

Companies should communicate how they are attempting to have a beneficial influence on the globe so that the general public may witness their pro-social efforts. Socially responsible businesses are much more essential to millennials and Generation Z. As more businesses see the influence of their socially and environmentally conscious initiatives on consumer perception, the more likely it is that they will follow suit. As a result of these two generations' purchasing perspectives, consumer attention has turned to social responsibility, particularly when it comes to the environment.

What are ethical *paradoxes in moral business philosophy?*

Ethical dilemmas, also known as ethical paradoxes in moral philosophy, are frequently evoked in an attempt to criticise or enhance an ethical theory or moral code in order to reconcile the contradiction. The necessity of ethical behaviour is emphasised by many organisations.

"An ethical dilemma is a circumstance in which a difficult decision must be made between two or more solutions, neither of which resolves the issue according to established ethical principles."

When faced with an ethical quandary, a person must choose a path of conduct that contradicts an established code of ethics or societal norms, such as laws and religious teachings, or their own moral beliefs about right and evil. Workplace pressures, on the other hand, can occasionally drive employees to engage in dubious practises. This is due to the fact that ethical challenges occur in a variety of shades of grey, not just black and white. There's also the issue of managerial pressure to fulfil predetermined goals on a regular basis. Organisations specify the means to attain these goals, but what counts is the ultimate result, and the employee may face an ethical issue. Consider the situation of a new account executive who is still learning the ropes. He had been jobless for months when he was eventually hired, via the good offices of a senior business development manager at an FMCG company. Within months, the teenagers were confronted with an ethical problem. His donor continued to provide him with invoices for a few thousand dollars, instructing him to edit them. The trainee was torn between his honesty and his gratitude, and he didn't know what to do. Months later, the trainee told the head office's chief accountant of the problem. This information was subsequently relayed to upper management. Surprisingly, the upper brass found themselves in a Catch-22 predicament! The senior manager was bringing in millions of dollars every month in business. Sacrificing him to save a few thousand rupees didn't seem like a good idea. Nonetheless, it had an influence on the integrity of the organisation. The problem was overcome by simply changing the rules.

According to a circular, expense invoices may no longer be filed directly to accounts.These should instead be sent through the department leader. That put a stop to the 'adjustments' as well as the employee's and employer's ethical dilemmas.

When we think of ethical difficulties, we think of things like open fraud, embezzlement, shady transactions, nepotism, and so on. Without a doubt, there are incidents of clear-cut ethical infractions. In that circumstance, any Ethics Committee or HR Head's job might be eliminated. To deter unethical behaviour, most professionally operated businesses have established codes of conduct. The ground rules are spelled out at the time employees are on boarded. The issue then becomes, How do you deal with such ethical dilemmas? There aren't any easy answers, to be sure. However, there are a few general principles to follow to help you negotiate such situations.

- It's common to throw problems under the rug in the hopes that everything will work out in the end. Unfortunately, it's possible that they won't. Remember that it only takes one lie to cover up a hundred. As a result, think about the consequences of reporting or not reporting the occurrence. Keep in mind that if anything goes wrong afterwards, you may have to deal with the consequences for the rest of your life. After evaluating these facts, take action.
- Putting off dealing with the problem won't help. It is preferable to figure out solutions to the problem as soon as possible. The longer the problem persists, the more difficult it becomes to resolve. It's also conceivable that the culprit is just putting himself out there. If you push back the first time, he or she is less likely to repeat the offence.
- If you're being ordered to do anything immoral, say something like, "If I'm not incorrect, I believe the

corporate regulations forbid such actions"—or something similar. Questioning the allocation of such a duty will make the manager feel uneasy, and he or she may decide to cancel the request rather than risk others finding out.

- Suggest some other ways to do the task without violating business policies. Again, refusing to comply with an unethical request will make your boss apprehensive about asking you to do anything similar in the future.
- Consult with coworkers or friends who have more expertise and can better advise you on how to handle the problem. They could recommend a different course of action to address your ethical quandary. Finally, if none of the options above work, take matters into your own hands.

Regardless of the outcome, decide if you want to blow the whistle and then take a stand. When it's evident that you're not going to breach the rules no matter what, top leaders who are promoting unethical agendas will often back off. Most of you are confronted with so-called ethical quandaries in your daily lives, and it will be critical to investigate the methods and means of developing the moral fibre that will allow you to overcome the difficulties of Catch-22 scenarios. If you were to define an ethical dilemma, you could say that it is a complicated circumstance including an apparent conceptual conflict between moral imperatives, in which obeying one would result in transgressing the other.

Let's have a peek at your work environment. Employees are inclined to do personal business on company time since they spend so much of their daily hours at work. Setting up doctor's appointments on company phone lines, making vacation reservations using their employer's computers and Internet connections, or even making phone calls for a freelance side business, stock market transactions, social work as an office bearer, and other personal work such as job searches, interviews, and so on, all while on company time and using company resources are examples of this. This ethical quandary appears to be rather obvious at first glance. Conducting personal business on company time may be considered an abuse or, at the very least, improper. There are, however, shades of grey here. What if your spouse calls to inform you that one of your children is unwell or that there is an emergency? Is it okay if you make a doctor's appointment or if you respond to an emergency? A decent rule of thumb for an employee is to ask his boss or the company's human resources department for clarity on what constitutes an actionable violation and what is not. The current accepted standard as defined by the code of conduct or ethical code can also provide valuable knowledge, and employees can be sensitised appropriately.

Employees frequently hide their true feelings due to the demands of their jobs, family concerns, job instability, and so on. Some people even accept harassment, and some people don't bother reporting unpleasant things like conduct, wrongdoings, unethical activities, and corruption because they are afraid of losing their employment. They are afraid that if they report harassment, wrongdoings, or unethical acts by a superior, they will be considered troublemakers and will suffer as a result. The ideal method to handle this ethical problem is for HR professionals to produce the company's employee handbook, which covers all elements and the intended action by the workers, rather than just interacting with them on a regular basis and feeling their pulse.

In both text and spirit, the same must be followed. It is their responsibility to add clear wording that states that reporting harassing behaviour, wrongdoing, or non-compliance with corporate policy and standards will not result in retaliation. You can continue to discuss the ethical difficulties that we confront in your daily lives. The golden rule is that remedial action must be taken where there are conscious pricks. It's a good idea to have a look at this quote.

"Ethics isn't about platitudes, let alone tautologies, logic, or mathematics; it's about tough choices or dilemmas." Martin Cohen

A more comprehensive approach to today's significant ethical challenges in the technology sector may help organisations stand out, safeguard their reputations, and better plan for and protect the future. There is no denying that the IT business has been a huge success. Our digital civilization is powered by its omnipresent goods and services. However, the industry's long-term ubiquity, scope, and impact have pushed it to confront a slew of unexpected and challenging ethical challenges. These difficulties were not necessarily caused by the IT sector, but many in the industry have reached a "convergence point" where they can no longer ignore them.As a result of big tech's perceived influence, sluggish regulation, and a lack of consistent industry norms, many customers, investors, employees, and governments are demanding greater general accountability from businesses.

In addition, the technology sector is becoming more self-aware, questioning its own ethical ideals and pondering how to properly control its growth and influence. It's commonly thought that the more power you have, the more responsibility you have to use it properly, regardless of who said it first. In an increasing number of sectors, the IT industry is being pushed to do more. Without a comprehensive approach to these challenges, IT businesses will be unable to address today's most pressing concerns while also failing to plan for tomorrow's. Technology businesses are being pushed to go above and above what is needed by law in terms of environmental sustainability. Some criticise the semiconductor industry for its energy use, inefficient supply chains, production waste, and water use in semiconductor manufacture. The good news is that technology organisations have enough market clout to effect meaningful change. Tech corporations are among the world's greatest users of renewable energy, and they're seeking to power their vast data centres with it. Some projects are centred on reducing waste, increasing recycling, and promoting circular economy ideas. Examples include Cisco's Takeback and Reuse initiative and Microsoft's 2030 zero waste objective. Others, such as Amazon's Climate Pledge, strive for net-zero carbon emissions.Apple, for example, has committed to being carbon-neutral across all of its companies by 2030. Threats to the truth include disinformation, misinformation, deepfakes, and the weaponization of data, which are being used by hordes of people and groups to attack, manipulate, and influence for personal benefit or to sow havoc. Technology businesses have encouraged governments to create legislation that clearly defines duties and standards in order to help solve this intractable problem. They're also working more closely with law enforcement and intelligence agencies, making public reports on their discoveries and stepping up their overall vigilance and action. These challenges are inextricably linked, and relying on separate responses to each may no longer be sufficient. It's likely that a transition to a more comprehensive approach is required.

The advantages of using a comprehensive approach might be enormous. It might help minimize negative publicity, consumer reaction, and regulatory action, lessen environmental harm, avoid legal issues, and prevent societal fragilities from worsening. It's not only about avoiding negative consequences; it's also about producing favourable ones.

According to the Deloitte Global 2021 Millennial and Generation Z Survey, over 70% of both millennials and Generation Z believe that corporations in general are more concerned with their own agendas than with the larger society. 20). Furthermore, just 47% of millennials believe business has a good influence on society. Finally, being able to demonstrate your ethical behaviour and offer examples to your clients may help you keep them.

Why does the battle against corruption is an important part of an organisation's ethics commitment?

Ethics and compliance are two distinct concepts that complement and strengthen one another. This commitment, however, must be backed up by precise rules and processes that will help the organisation optimize its efforts to remove corruption from corporate activities. Third parties, elaborate montages, concealed conflicts of interest, and so on are all examples of corruption. It's crucial to specify exactly what behaviour is and isn't acceptable.

Specific dangers should be addressed via the use of suitable measures and behaviour. Together, these procedures make up the company's anti-corruption compliance program, which allows it to demonstrate its commitment to ethical business practises. When backed up by a well-executed compliance program, stated pledges to ethics become meaningful. On the other hand, an anti-corruption compliance program by itself will not suffice. If a member of employees is hell-bent on evading anti-corruption compliance laws and procedures, he or she will find a way. There might be a variety of motivations: personal gain, a kickback from the bribe taker, or just an easier way to meet sales targets and earn incentives. Only an organisation, clear stance on ethical business practises, along with a comprehensive program, can prevent an individual from acting corruptly. For greatest efficacy, ethics necessitates compliance processes, and compliance procedures necessitate ethics.

It doesn't matter if the position is called "Ethics Officer" or "Compliance Officer." What matters is that the person assigned to this position understands that an anti-corruption compliance program must be backed by a strong desire to conduct business ethically and that ethical business practises are more effectively pursued when backed by a strong anti-corruption compliance program. Some businesses hire an Ethics & Compliance Officer, while others hire an Ethics Officer and a Compliance Officer, and still others hire a Business Compliance Officer and a Legal Compliance Officer. The company's decision to choose the path that best respects the company's history, organisation, and core business is far more essential than the position's label. In difficult settings, compliance initiatives can provide a competitive edge. A good compliance program, on the other hand, needs a business culture that values integrity and ethical behaviour in order to maximise that advantage. It's worth noting that one of the most well-known American groups dedicated to this topic is called the "Society for Corporate Ethics and Compliance," which emphasises that experts feel the two are inexorably linked, even though the issues and techniques of compliance and ethics differ. The following points are to be considered while establishing OEC desk in your organisation:

- Increase the number of in-person conversations to better understand difficulties.
- Invite individuals to tell the unvarnished truth; this aids in the dismantling of organisational silos.
- To discover and then root out hidden hazards, ask the correct questions of the right individuals.
- To get workers‘ attention, they published anonymised, sanitised examples.
- Communicate ethical guidelines in a unique way to ensure that they are imprinted on the mind for the rest of one's life.
- Make a positive first impression with HR during onboarding.
- OEC's internal branding includes an intranet, desktop branding, and a learning management system (LMS).
- Obtain the CEO's and upper management's support. To avoid compliance fatigue, send reminders on a frequent basis.
- To minimise training weariness, create a calendar for a yearly multiple training program and make sure you're making the most of your learners' time.
- To make OEC intervention more meaningful and effective, use risk or role-based training.
- Through a mobile application, they promote microlearning, bite-size learning, and burst learning methods.

- Develop local trainers, such as managers, for a long-term training program.
- Inform your employees about cyber security and the dangers of social media.
- Hire a third-party study team to evaluate the existing situation or operational flaws.
- Appoint a third-party audit to eliminate any potential prejudice.
- Emphasize the necessity of anonymous reporting in order to avoid future business risks.
- Create a hotline to swiftly obtain first-hand information.
- Creating a dashboard for current procedures and a report on their progress to share with the CEO
- Reduce your COBC certification procedure and encourage all employees to participate in quarterly certifications.
- Create a document library and an online bank of all sorts of SR applications and forms for Ethics and Compliance.
- Real-time regulatory needs should be reflected in policy.
- It is necessary to guarantee that concerns about ethics and compliance are properly examined, monitored, handled, and addressed.
- Ascertain that programs for measuring efficiency and identifying possible areas for improvement are in place.

How far may ethical difficulties in an organisation be challenging for any business owner to handle?

Though there are rules and legislation in place to hold employees and employers accountable, they do not completely prohibit people from acting unethically. According to the 2019 Global Business Ethics Survey, 25% of employees believe that their top managers do not grasp critical ethical and regulatory business risks throughout the corporation. Ethical concerns in business cover a wide range of topics that fall under the purview of an organisation's ethical standards.

Fundamental ethical challenges in business include supporting honesty and trust-based behaviour, but more sophisticated issues include accommodating diversity, empathic decision-making, and compliance and governance that is compatible with the organisation's fundamental principles. According to the 2019 Global Business Ethics Survey, 25% of employees still believe that their top managers lack integrity. Long-held views that have been shown to be effective in the past may need to be altered. With a more ethical approach, there will likely be greater dialogue and transparency regarding the trade-offs between efficiency and performance.

- It is critical to find skilled ethical specialists who can advise the business while also understanding human behavior, prejudice, and unanticipated consequences.
- Existing corporate structures may have difficulties retaining both cash streams and good ethical principles.
- It's possible that a thorough ethical strategy may be more costly. It may take longer to design software and products that are fully aware of the true consequences.
- Engineering procedures may need to be altered.
- It may be necessary to establish new methods for evaluating, recognising, and rewarding executives, employees, and project teams.
- Technology Businesses should no longer be focused only on growth and be competent at business. They should think about the ethical implications of their actions in a systematic way to better navigate the grey zones and avoid unintended effects in the future.

Finally, it's not only about developing ethical and trustworthy technology; it's also about making it easier for the entire sector to make ethical and trustworthy judgments. Taking a comprehensive approach to the sector's ethical challenges and fostering foresight and a systems perspective will help assure a more sustainable industry and foster long-term trust with consumers, partners, employees, governments, and the general public. This is true not only for today's problems, but also for those that will inevitably arise in the future. Examine instances of ethical dilemmas to learn how you could approach these challenging circumstances. Managers are put to the test in the workplace when faced with the task of addressing an ethical problem. Certain instances frequently fall outside of the scope of processes or the formal code of conduct, putting managers under pressure. The challenge with ethical decision-making is that no one option can be made in isolation; each decision has an impact on a number of others, and the goal is to strike a balance to arrive at a win-win situation. Though there are no hard and fast rules for resolving ethical concerns, managers can take a number of steps to do so. Because of the growing use of social media, employees' online behaviour has become a determinant in their job status. The ethics of terminating or disciplining employees for their internet postings is a tricky issue. However, when an employee's online activity is taken into account, a boundary is frequently drawn.

However, when an employee's online activity is seen to be disloyal to their company, a boundary is frequently drawn. This implies that a Facebook post complaining about work is not unlawful in and of itself, but it can be punished if it causes a decrease in business. Similarly, business owners must be able to appreciate and not penalise employees who act as whistleblowers to regulatory authorities or on social media. This means that workers should be encouraged to raise awareness of workplace breaches online rather than penalised for doing so. Any firm must follow proper bookkeeping procedures. "Cooking the books" and other unethical accounting practises are severe concerns for organisations, particularly publicly listed companies.

To manage ethical concerns in business that occur in your organisation, you must first have a complete awareness of what those difficulties might entail. Understanding how to recognize and, more importantly, prevent these issues from becoming a problem will help you keep your emphasis on business development and success rather than correction. There is no one-size-fits-all solution for businesses when they begin to establish a comprehensive strategy. These challenges can be daunting when they are considered as a whole, and there is no obvious road ahead. It will very certainly need a commitment to numerous orthodoxies throughout an organisation's culture, financial plans, and operational procedures, as well as a willingness to confront them.

- There are three key ideas in ethical decision-making that may be applied to solve problems. These are the three principles of intuitionism, moral idealism, and utilitarianism.
- The intuition principle operates on the idea that the HR person or management is knowledgeable enough to see the gravity of the issue and act appropriately, so that the final choice does not cause harm to any individual concerned, directly or indirectly.

- The principle of moral idealism, on the other hand, maintains that there is a clear contrast between what is good and what is terrible, and that this is true in all cases.
- Moral decisions must be considered before being made, rather than being taken at face value. It's a great idea to make up hypothetical situations, create case studies, and then engage others in brainstorming on the same. This sheds some light on previously undisclosed issues and broadens the scope of comprehension and logical decision-making.
- The management uses the balance sheet technique to lay out the benefits and drawbacks of the decision. This aids in gaining a clearer view of things and better arranging them.
- One useful approach is to state one's position on various ethical concerns clearly and send a clear message to all members of the organisation, especially those who are more vulnerable to unethical actions. As a result, employees will be less likely to use unethical methods as a result of this.
- Integrating moral decision-making and developing a strategic management plan. Morality and ethics are frequently discussed issues, and ethical perfection is practically impossible to acquire.
- Integrating ethical decision-making into organisational strategic management is a better strategy to cope with this. The method by which the HR manager obtains a viewpoint that differs from the typical employee- or stakeholder-oriented viewpoint.

Taking a comprehensive approach to ethical challenges, if done well, may promote market distinction and disruption. The strategy might be used to better recruit and retain new generations of talent. You might be able to retain more consumers if you increase your customer retention.Admitting that your firm has an "ethics issue" may be the first hurdle to overcome. In a poll of technology professionals conducted by Deloitte, 82% strongly believed that their organisation was ethical. Only 24% strongly agreed that the IT industry has an ethical approach to the goods and services it develops. At present, taking a comprehensive approach to ethical challenges may appear to be someone else's concern.

An organisational Ombudsman gives opportunities for people with problems to bring their complaints forward securely and effectively. Ombudsperson is a source of new issue discovery and early warning, as well as systemic reform ideas to enhance existing systems. Most people are aware that whistleblowers are frequently punished and retaliated against. Ethical executives strive to safeguard and enhance the company's good name and employee morale by engaging in no activity that may be seen as disrespectful to others. Developing a culture of integrity and ethics in organisations is one strategy to guarantee those values are preserved. Sexual harassment is unwanted sexual behaviour that causes a person to feel insulted, embarrassed, or intimated management system for female employees in the public and commercial sectors to document and resolve sexual harassment complaints.

Every regulated organisation now needs a solid ethics and corporate compliance program. The readiness of a business to deal with a compliance issue is crucial since it affects brand value and revenue. Being proactive also necessitates collaboration between the corporate compliance team and other departments and regulatory compliance groups.

Strong cultures are defined by a high degree of agreement about what is valued and a high level of intensity about those values. Naysayers can stymie the organisation's operations by causing barriers. Good conduct is rewarded, but it is also evident that poor behaviour may have negative effects. When faced with an ethical quandary, a person must choose a path of conduct that contradicts an established code of ethics.

A more comprehensive approach to today's significant ethical challenges in the technology sector may help organisations safeguard their reputations and better plan for and protect the future. Ethical concerns in business cover a wide range of topics that fall under the purview of an organisation's ethical standards. There are no hard and fast rules for resolving ethical concerns, but managers can take a number of steps to do so. There is no one-size-fits-all solution for businesses when they begin to establish a comprehensive strategy. Integrating ethical decision-making into organisational strategic management is a better strategy to cope with this. The strategy might be used to better recruit and retain new generations of talent.

"In addition to the altruistic aspects, a corporate social responsibility program may help organisations differentiate themselves from their competition. Enhanced brand image, higher media coverage, improved consumer loyalty, and additional investment prospects are just a few of the advantages."

- Dr. Amit Das

CHAPTER THREE

Corporate Culture Is The Epicentre Of Strong Compliance And Conscientiousness

"Play fair, be prepared for others to play dirty, and don't let them drag you into the mud."- Richard Branson

It's easy to ignore the fundamentals that serve as a solid basis for individuals and businesses to develop and thrive. Ethics and integrity are examples of necessities. The problem is that ethics and integrity have never been more vital. Sure, easy but dishonest paths to success might enable organisations and entrepreneurs to earn a quick profit and perhaps enjoy some temporary glory.

However, sustainable businesses that succeed in difficult times and leave a legacy are all about doing the right thing year after year, through difficult and easy times, change, and volatility. Ethics provides a moral compass for organisations, their executives, and their workforce. They ensure that the most critical policies and commercial choices are not only profitable but also fair, unbiased, and honest. Over time, ethics have an impact on a brand's outward reputation as well as its internal culture.

What is Corporate Governance?

Did you know that almost 40% of businesses are impacted by some form of maladministration? This can include financial fraud, corruption, industrial espionage, fraud, theft, embezzlement, bullying, or even sexual harassment. Damages of more than 100,000 euros are not uncommon. 90% of all whistleblowers attempt to resolve observed issues internally before contacting authorities, the media, or the public - assuming they discover appropriate channels and an open culture within the company?

"Corporate governance is a system of rules, regulations, and processes that regulate the direction and control of an organisation. Corporate governance encompasses the relationships between the many stakeholders as well as the goals for which the organisation is managed."

Corporate governance is the use of best management practises, strict respect of the word and spirit of the law, and adherence to ethical standards for successful wealth management and distribution. When there is a separation of ownership and control, corporate governance refers to the collection of systems that impact the decisions made by management. The Board of Directors, institutional shareholders, and the functioning of the market for corporate control are examples of these monitoring systems.

Corporate governance refers to how a corporation is run to guarantee that all of its stakeholders receive a fair share of the company's profits and assets. This chapter delves into the major issues that the compliance department encounters in its pursuit of 100% compliance. I will discuss how technology solutions and good practises can help to mitigate the risk of non-compliance, from developing training programmes and messages that effectively embed the appropriate behaviours to creating a compliance culture and eliminating administration headaches around compliance monitoring.

"Good corporate governance entails an organisation's commitment to operating its operations in a lawful, ethical, and transparent manner—a commitment that must start at the top and spread across the organisation."

Corporate governance is a system of rules, policies, and processes that guide the Board of Directors and independent committees in their monitoring and management of an organisation. It entails balancing the needs of an organisation's stakeholders, which include management, workers, suppliers, customers, and the community, with the requirement to produce value for its shareholders and owners. Having a solid, active governance programme is essential for an organisation's long-term financial health, development, and success.

"Corporate Governance is the application of best management practices, Compliance of law in true letter and spirit and adherence to ethical standards for effective management and distribution of wealth and discharge of social responsibility for sustainable development of all stakeholders."-Institute of Company Secretaries of India

Corporate governance makes businesses more responsible and transparent to investors, and it equips them with the tools they need to address genuine stakeholder concerns, including long-term environmental and social development. Increased access to finance promotes new investments, boosts economic growth, and creates job possibilities, all of which contribute to development.

"The decent behaviour and sound judgement of individuals in charge of operating an organisation are crucial to successful governance."

Corporate governance is to create an organisation that optimises shareholder wealth. It envisions an organisation that prioritises satisfying social commitments to stakeholders over maximising profits. Shareholders, debt holders, trade creditors, suppliers, consumers, and communities affected by the corporation's activity are the primary external stakeholder groups in today's corporations. Any of the policies and practises that managean organisation can be referred to as corporate governance, but that definition falls short of describing what corporate governance actually is. It's more accurate to state that "governance" refers to the policies and procedures that enable the company to achieve its objectives while avoiding unnecessary conflicts. Shareholders, board members, consumers, and the many communities inside an enterprise (Executive Management, Operations, Project Management, Process Improvement, Information Technology, and so on) all have different demands that must be balanced. When done well, governance fosters an open, honest atmosphere that supports structure in planning and execution and encourages board members and executive committees to invest in the corporation's ability to innovate and expand.

How to develope a strong corporate culture that encourages compliance?

one of the most crucial competitive advantages an organisation may have is a strong corporate culture. A strong culture not only promotes improved employee performance and engagement, but it also lays the groundwork for a stronger compliance program—a critical pillar of a healthy and well-run organisation.

The corporate governance framework is made up of explicit and implicit contracts between the company and stakeholders for the distribution of responsibilities, rights, and rewards; procedures for resolving stakeholders' sometimes conflicting interests based on their duties, privileges, and roles; and procedures for proper supervision, control, and information-flows to serve as a system of checks and balances. It has to do with the corporate structure's complexity, notably the growth of group entities like subsidiaries, associates, joint ventures, and special-purpose corporations, which are typically piled on top of one another. Boards of Directors of group entities below the parent frequently have relatively limited governance responsibilities, and these entities are often out of the sight of the group Board of Directors and senior management. I will tell you how companies and regulators must concentrate on group governance concerns as well as the governance and management of supply chain business partners.

The management of a corporation's relationships with its management, Board of Directors, shareholders, and other stakeholders The provision of a framework through which the company's objectives are established, as well as the monitoring of the tools employed to achieve these objectives, including performance monitoring in this respect, increases the openness of the company's decision-making processes. The provision of appropriate incentives for the Board of Directors and management to achieve goals that are in the best interests of the corporation and its shareholders. Risk management and the reduction of the consequences of commercial misadventure is a large part of how a corporation is governed and controlled, which is determined by its ownership structure.

"Corporate governance is to operate the business in line with the owner or shareholder's objective, which is normally to earn as much money as possible while conforming to the basic principles of society incorporated into legislation and local customs."- Friedman

Good governance practises are influenced by the organisation's culture and attitude, as well as the individuals in control. Corporate governance is a value-based framework for doing business in a fair and transparent manner. In all of its transactions, it assures accountability, openness, and justice, and it satisfies the expectations of all stakeholders. Diverse components should be communicated to various stakeholders in a timely and accurate manner.

Corporate governance is the practise of adhering to ethical norms for successful wealth management and distribution, as well as accepting social responsibility for the long-term growth of all stakeholders, including consumers, workers, and society as a whole. Corporate governance is the set of processes, practises, policies, rules, regulations, and laws that regulate how corporations are conducted in the best interests of their stakeholders.

Corporate governance is concerned with respecting the law's spirit rather than merely the text. Corporate governance standards should go above and beyond what is required by law. Corporate governance refers to the act of communicating honestly and transparently to the outside world about how the organisation operates on the inside. By delegating decision-making to appropriate management levels, corporate governance creates checks and balances in decision-making.

Corporate governance, in other words, should be an integrated component of the decision-making process. Corporate governance can be accomplished through the use of best legal and managerial practices, ethics, wealth creation management, and foresight.

Corporate governance is an important instrument for protecting and maximising the long-term wealth of shareholders. Thus, corporate governance can be defined as an approach in which corporations are managed in an ethical, accountable, transparent, and fair manner, with a blend of legal and management practises to imbed the same in the decision-making process of an organisation and to communicate the same accurately and timely, in such a way that both stakeholders' expectations and legal standards are not only met, but the corporations try to exceed them.

Would you like to know more about Corporate Governance philosophy of Indian blue chip organisation?

Corporate governance is a collection of procedures and practises that guarantee that an organisation's affairs are handled in a way that promotes accountability, transparency, and fairness in all of its transactions in the broadest sense and meets its stakeholders' ambitions and societal expectations. It requires professionals to raise their competency and capability levels to meet the expectations of managing the enterprise and its resources effectively with the highest standards of ethics.

"Corporate governance is a journey for continuously improving sustainable value creation and is an upward moving target."

Corporate governance is a system of procedures, practises, policies, rules, regulations, and laws by which corporations are directed, managed, and administered by management in the best interests of stakeholders. It ensures the fairness, openness, accountability, and integrity of management. Corporate governance is more of a way of life than a legal requirement. is more of a manner of life than a legal requirement. Corporate governance is the application of ethical norms to the successful management and distribution of wealth, as well as the fulfilment of social duty for the long-term development of all stakeholders, including consumers, workers, and society. Corporate governance is the strict adherence to the text and spirit of the law, rules, and regulations.

"Corporate governance establishes clear benchmarks against which responsibility's performance can be assessed."

Corporate governance is a comprehensive mechanism that directs and controls organisations in order to improve their wealth-generating ability. Because major corporations consume a significant amount of social resources, the governance process should ensure that these resources are used in a way that meets the goals of stakeholders and society's expectations. Any genuine corporate governance policy must empower the company's top management. At the same time, governance must establish a system of checks and balances to guarantee that the executive management's decision-making abilities are used with care and responsibility in order to satisfy stakeholders' ambitions and social expectations. Trusteeship, openness, empowerment, responsibility, control, and ethical corporate citizenship are the foundations of corporate governance philosophy.

Corporate governance aids in the achievement of corporate goals by establishing a framework within which stakeholders may most effectively pursue the organisation's goals. Corporate governance refers to management's acknowledgement of shareholders' inalienable rights as the genuine owners of the company, as well as their own position as trustees on their behalf.

"Corporate governance ensures principles, ethical corporate practises, openness, and disclosures in accordance with legal regulations and norms."

Good corporate governance practises are defined by an organisation's solid commitment to and implementation of ethical procedures in all of its dealings with a diverse collection of stakeholders. Corporate governance extends beyond legal requirements and is rooted in fundamental corporate principles and values that must be followed in word and spirit.

Good corporate governance standards are also necessary for a long-term business strategy that generates value for all of the company's stakeholders. It is focused on the implementation of open procedures and approaches. It is concerned about the high levels of disclosure required for disseminating corporate, financial, and operational information to all stakeholders.

"Corporate governance is concerned with establishing a well-defined corporate structure with checks and balances and delegating decision-making to appropriate levels of management."

Corporate governance is a value-based framework for doing business in a fair and transparent manner. The goal of the corporate governance framework is to provide responsibility in all aspects of business and to use democratic and open methods. Corporate governance is concerned with upholding the spirit of the law rather than the letter of the law. Corporate governance standards should go above and beyond what is required by law. Corporate governance entails communicating the company's internal operations to the public in an open and honest way. Management is the trustee, not the owner, of the capital of the shareholders.

"Transparency is important to Corporate Governance, thus it maintains a high level of information."

Compliance with legal and regulatory standards is just part of good company governance. Good governance enables the bank to more effectively manage and oversee its operations, as well as maintain a high level of corporate ethics and maximise value for all of its stakeholders.

The goal of corporate governance is to protect and enhance shareholder value, as well as the interests of other stakeholders such as customers, employees, and society at large, to ensure transparency and integrity in communication and to make full, accurate, and clear information available to all parties involved, to ensure accountability for performance and customer service, and to achieve excellence at all levels, and to provide corporate leadership. Establishing properly written and transparent management procedures for policy creation, implementation, review, decision-making, monitoring, control, and reporting are all part of corporate governance.

Corporate governance is a critical component of increasing efficiency, growth, and investor trust. As a good corporate citizen, the company should be committed to sound corporate practises based on awareness, openness, fairness, professionalism, and accountability in order to gain the trust of its many stakeholders and pave the way for long-term success.

Going beyond the letter of the law in sustaining corporate governance standards; maintaining openness and a high level of disclosure making a distinct distinction between personal convenience and business resources;

communicating internally in a genuine way maintaining a basic and transparent corporate structure that is exclusively driven by business demands in all countries where the firm operates; adopting a trusteeship model in which management, rather than being the owner, is the trustee of the shareholders' money.

In today's globalised financial markets, this is extremely important. Companies may borrow money from a much bigger pool of investors because of international capital flows. Corporate governance structures must be trustworthy, widely understood across borders, and adhere to globally accepted norms if enterprises and governments are to realise the full benefits of the global capital market and attract long-term capital. Even if corporations do not primarily rely on foreign sources of capital, a credible corporate governance framework backed by effective supervision and enforcement mechanisms will help boost domestic investor confidence, lower capital costs, support the smooth operation of financial markets, and ultimately attract more stable sources of funding.

The corporate governance structure should encourage open and fair markets as well as efficient resource allocation. It should adhere to the rule of law and promote effective oversight and enforcement. Effective corporate governance necessitates a stable legal, regulatory, and institutional framework on which market actors may depend when forming private contractual relationships.

This corporate governance framework usually consists of aspects of legislation, regulation, self-regulatory frameworks, voluntary pledges, and company practises that are based on a country's unique circumstances, history, and tradition. As a result, the ideal balance of law, regulation, self-regulation, volunteer norms, and other factors will differ from country to country. Soft law aspects based on the "comply or explain" concept, such as corporate governance codes, can be productively supplemented by legislative and regulatory parts of the corporate governance framework to allow for flexibility and address the specificities of individual organisations.

"What works effectively in one firm, for one investor, or for one stakeholder may not be relevant to other corporations, investors, or stakeholders operating in a different environment and under different conditions."

The various aspects of the corporate governance framework should be examined and, if required, updated when new experiences and business conditions arise. Proper governance takes time and consideration from dedicated leaders who see the value of coordinating all levels of a business to achieve desired outcomes. More than ever, board members and other corporate executives must be prepared to deal with unprecedented levels of uncertainty. The global economic landscape is evolving as a result of increased globalisation, technological proliferation, and the increased urgency around climate change and biodiversity loss.

In the face of the COVID-19 epidemic, board members and other corporate executives are obligated to confront these issues. Without a doubt, the negative consequences of these complicated events signal that a major overhaul of corporate governance is not just essential, but also demanded – and business executives must be ready.

Is there any adavantage of having good Corporate Governance in an organisation?

Corporate governance guarantees thatan organisation's environment is fair and transparent, and that workers may be held responsible for their activities. Poor corporate governance, on the other hand, leads to waste, mismanagement, and corruption. Only excellent governance can ensure lasting and reliable commercial performance, regardless of the type of endeavour.

Accountability, fairness, openness, assurance, leadership, and stakeholder management are the cornerstones of good corporate governance. All six are necessary for an organisation's performance and the development of strong professional relationships with its stakeholders, which include board members, managers, workers, customers, regulators, and, most significantly, shareholders.

- Corporate governance is balancing the interests ofan organisation's many stakeholders, including shareholders, management, customers, suppliers, financiers, the government, and the general public.
- It provides proper transparency and effective decision-making in order to meet company objectives.
- Compliance with regulations and laws is aided by corporate governance.
- It promotes greater transparency in commercial transactions.
- It ensures that ideals are upheld and that business is conducted in an ethical manner.
- At the head of affairs, a governing body capable of making independent and impartial judgments is in place.
- The govening body oversees non-executive and independent Directors in order to protect shareholders' interests.
- The governing body follows open procedures and bases its decisions on accurate and complete data.

- It has influence over important changes that affect the firm.
- Governing body successfully controls and monitors the company's affairs as well as the management team's activities.
- It builds morale, a reputation, and a legacy. Putting in place procedures that promote good governance strengthensan organisation's identity, allowing stakeholders and potential investors to place greater faith in it, allowing you to form better long-term partnerships.

- It increases the financial performance success rate and improves sustainability.
- It increases the capacity to recruit and retain talent. A lot of emphasis has been placed on culture as a major contributor toan organisation's success.
- Maintaining openness in areas such as fairness, accountability, and operations provides your employees with a better feeling of responsibility and knowledge of their role in creating value inside the company.
- It creates an efficient framework for achieving corporate goals and Major stakeholders such as workers, suppliers, and the community have all been considered in decision-making, resulting in a broader vision for successful outcomes. Providing each stakeholder with a proportion of useful engagement fosters a more responsible culture, increasing the likelihood of achieving organisational goals.
- It increases your chances of gaining a competitive advantage. It creates investment opportunities. An organisation that symbolises stability and dependability has a higher chance of attracting premium investors as

well as a better chance of borrowing money at a lower cost.

- It provides a practical framework for all stages of decision-making: The capacity to make well-informed judgments may boost productivity and mitigate the consequences of future errors. Ensuring that information is easily available to important stakeholders, i.e., a culture of transparency, is one strategy to encourage this type of decision-making skill.
- Strong corporate governance standards may improve the effectiveness and efficiency of business operations by instilling values throughout the organisation, which has the potential to generate significant advantages.
- It creates investment opportunities. An organisation that symbolises stability and dependability has a higher chance of attracting premium investors as well as a better chance of borrowing money at a lower cost.
- It provides a practical framework for all stages of decision-making. The capacity to make well-informed judgments may boost productivity and mitigate the consequences of future errors. Ensuring that information is easily available to important stakeholders, i.e., a culture of transparency, is one strategy to encourage this type of decision-making skill.

Corporate governance, as the name indicates, relates to how a business chooses to govern itself, and it is underpinned by a system of rules that provide direction and control in order to achieve its objectives. The continuous implementation of these rules and principles strives to build a healthy, compliant, transparent, and accountable corporate culture that is regularly examined and developed in order to guarantee that your behaviour matches the values your company aspires to reflect, among other things.

The deployment of a strong governance protocol is designed to help with the capacity to swiftly detect concerns and make quick choices to remedy them, hence lowering the chance of a crisis and the expenses associated with it. Every industry is continually developing or has the potential to do so in the future. It is vital to ensure that your organisation is adaptive to change and that you create an atmosphere where your practises can be perpetuated if you want to maintain a competitive edge and a chance of survival.

Corporations require robust governance frameworks that provide them with the tools they need to mitigate risk and make sound choices. Board members, steering executives, and managers should all understand their duties and how they fit into the larger organisational structure oncean organisation has established its governance guidelines. Each person's role is solidified via governance, ensuring that they do not stray from the purpose. Proper governance structures explain the rules and methods for making corporate decisions, as well as the allocation of rights and obligations among different members in the business.

"Any corporation without governance is like a railway without a track. No matter how much potential the company has, it will never go through the necessary business transformation to get to where it wants to go since it has nothing to guide it."

Airbnb Co-Founder and CEO Brian Chesky, a new-age internet entrepreneur, has established Airbnb, one of the hottest travel enterprises of our time. Although he received some negative press for allegedly breaking out-of-date laws that did not account for the new connected, sharing economy, Airbnb has also been responsible for generating income, engaging and including local communities in a rapidly growing travel industry, and encouraging local experiences and integration as opposed to corporate-run, standardised, and cookie-cutter hotel experiences.

Brian spoke out against Airbnb hosts who discriminate against people based on their ethnicity or sexual orientation. Brian, as a corporate citizen, also stood out against Trump's visa ban and gave free housing to refugees during this trying time. His remarks, and the actions that support them, reflect the open, honest, and positive culture that he is attempting to establish not just within the organisation, but also among the travel industry as a whole. When it comes to developing Airbnb, Brian has been known to prioritise values and culture before growth and money. The end product has been spectacular. Honesty and ethics are not even options for Brian. What is unique about you that every other person would want to know about you?

"Integrity, honesty - those aren't just basic principles, those are the kinds of ideals that everyone should have. There must be three, five, or six things that are distinctively yours."-Brian Chesky

Efficiency will suffer if leadership is poisonous. The leadership and governance given by those at the top will have a big impact on how well these risks are managed. Enron, FIFA, and The News of the World are just a few instances of companies where poor leadership contributed to widespread unethical behaviour. When things go wrong, however, top leaders nearly always find it incredibly difficult to detouch themselves.

It's not every day that a job advertisement catches the attention of the press. Every day, a merger or acquisition takes place somewhere. However, owing to Satyam's projected image, co-players in the market are abandoning their ambitions to acquire the company. If the industry can rebuild the faith of the same investors that Satyam duped, the company's corporate governance failure may encourage competitors to pursue market share generated by its aftermath.

What makes a corporate governance programme effective in terms of increasingan organisation's chances of success rather than failure?

You have seen several examples of poor governance procedures leading to considerable market value depreciation throughout history. You witnessed it in 2001, when Enron was wiped out by a well-publicised accounting scam. You saw it again in 2014, when GM's inability to heed a whistleblower's warnings about its faulty ignition switches resulted in fines, penalties, and settlements totaling more than $2 billion. Wells Fargo workers, customers, and shareholders have lately been impacted by investigations into aggressive product cross-selling practises and misleading brokerage clients about trading high-fee debt products.

A lack of corporate governance may result in economic loss, corruption, and a damaged image, not only for the company, but for society as a whole, or even worse, for the entire world. This type of corporate governance is also intended to reduce risk and eliminate corrosive components insidean organisation. Education, tighter accounting controls, corporate governance, transparency, and disclosure are some of the areas of improvement and ways countries can maintain their leading position in the financial markets so that minorities and foreign countries can invest and exercise greater oversight over corporations.

According to the story, two weavers offer an emperor a new suit of clothing that is invisible to people who are unsuited for their positions, ignorant, or inept. No one dares to declare they don't see any suit of clothing on the emperor as he parades before his subjects in his new attire for fear of being labelled "unfit for their positions, ignorant, or inept." "But he isn't wearing anything at all!" a youngster finally exclaims. Everyone begins to laugh and point to the naked monarch. It also makes statutory disclosures and notifies any parties who may be impacted by its decisions. You may not realise the significance of this child's story until many years later. It describes how boards of Directors, executive management teams, and other commercial groupings, although made up of mostly good people, can operate fraudulently or corruptly.

Unfortunately, corporate governance did not receive much attention until the Sarbanes-Oxley Act was enacted into law by President Bush in 2002. The Act included a slew of changes aimed at enhancing corporate accountability and preventing financial fraud. Changes imposed by the Act may not have seemed significant at the time, but extensive fraud that bankrupted Enron and WorldCom caused significant market upheaval. Whether we're talking about trading, financial, corruption, environmental, or safety-related scandals, they frequently arise in companies with corporate cultures that prioritise profits over ethics, safety, or the environment.

With the right corporate culture, the Deepwater Horizon environmental disaster, Takata's airbag failure, Tepco's nuclear power plant disaster, GM's ignition switch failure, Olympus and Toshiba's accounting scandals, Volkwagen's emissions scandal, and GlaxoSmithKline's and Leighton Holdings' bribery scandals would not have happened. Many investors were concerned that if organisations continued to mismanage their assets and investments, they would lose money.

The Sarbanes-Oxley Act gave investors a sense of security. Proper governance, on the other hand, is no longer only about investor protection; it is now a must for organisations to prosper. Project management and company reform efforts fail more frequently without adequate governance, making potential investors hesitant. According to the Enron story, every time you turn a stone, another worm emerges. That appears to be the tale of the Enron scandal. Not a day goes by without a fresh revelation of corporate wrongdoing, and one begins to question if there is anything in our enterprise's protocols and structure that can avoid such a disaster.

Enron is a good illustration of how individuals at the top permitted a culture of secrecy, rule-breaking, and fraudulent behaviour to thrive. It also had a task group for corporate social responsibility and a code of conduct in the areas of security, human rights, social investment, and public participation. Despite this, no one obeyed the rules. The Board of Directors openly permitted management to violate the code, particularly when the CFO was permitted to serve on special-purpose entities (SPEs); the audit committee permitted suspect accounting practises while making no attempt to investigate SPE transactions; and the auditors failed to prevent questionable accounting. It has co-filed a shareholder petition in response to concerns that Wal-Mart Stores Inc., the US supermarket conglomerate, is not adhering to its own corporate governance requirements. Karina Litvack is the Director of governance and long-term investment. Despite having robust rules on paper, Wal-Mart has had difficulty implementing them across its US operations. As a consequence of the company's unwillingness to engage in a fruitful debate about how it develops and promotes a compliance culture, they have joined a worldwide coalition of significant filers led by the New York City Employees' Retirement System in filing a shareholder proposal.

What might be the cause of such a massive collapse?

It's one of corporate India's worst unfolding chapters. The organisation's top-level management underestimated the severity of the gangrene. The function of the auditors is also being questioned, as is how such a large-scale financial wrongdoing could have gone undiscovered. A business will always have two sides; it is not required to make profits all of the time, but it is vital to maintain the integrity of the firm. Workplace stress can reducean organisation's productivity.

How do businesses interpret the statutory part of Corporate Governance?

The higher the degree of corporate governance, the more powerful the corporation is from the perspective of its shareholders. The active and independent Directors are the ones who inject and contribute to portraying the company as one with a good perspective. Corporate governance laws in India compel corporations to audit their working culture and provide a more favourable picture to the shareholder community since their activities have several legal ramifications. The new rules, which came into effect after the Companies Act of 2013, are highly balanced. Shareholders are involved in company decision-making, and numerous protections have been implemented to ensure that the interests of shareholders and society as a whole are not overlooked. Corporate governance fosters the much-needed openness in businesses. As a result, it propels India forward in the global race of growing economies.

Corporate governance is dependent on the integrity and effectiveness of the financial markets. Poor corporate governance limitsan organisation's potential and can result in financial difficulties and fraud. Companies with good governance outperform their competition and attract investors who can help fund future growth. The Principles of Corporate Governance, issued by the Organisation for Economic Cooperation and Development in 1999, have since become a global benchmark for governments, investors, corporations, and other stakeholders. They've also been adopted as one of the Financial Stability Board's Key Standards for Sound Financial Systems, and they serve as the basis for the World Bank's Corporate Governance Reports on Standards and Codes Compliance (ROSC).

On April 22, 2004, the OECD announced an updated version of the OECD Principles of Corporate Governance. It includes a lot of new ideas as well as revisions to old ones. Members of the OECD and representatives from OECD and non-OECD countries participated in a consultation process. The OECD's regional corporate governance roundtables in Latin America, Asia, the Middle East, and North Africa, as well as experts, an online public consultation, and the OECD's official advisory bodies, the Business and Industry Advisory Committee (BIAC) and the Trade Union Advisory Committee, conducted a second review of the principles in 2014/15, based on the 2004 version of the principles (TUAC).

Businesses should ensure that they have systems in place to resolve any possible conflicts of interest and offer a framework for internal complaints regarding management or board appointments, according to the OECD guidelines.an organisation's management, Board of Directors, shareholders, and other stakeholders are all involved in corporate governance. Corporate governance also establishes the framework within which the company's goals are created, as well as the methods for achieving those goals and measuring success.

The principles are meant to be simple, easy to grasp, and accessible to the international community. The role of government, semi- government, and private sector initiatives is to assess the quality of the corporate governance framework and develop more detailed mandatory or voluntary provisions that can take into account country-specific economic, legal, and cultural differences based on the principles.

The Principles apply to both financial and non-financial publicly traded organisations. They may also be a valuable instrument for improving corporate governance in organisations whose shares are not publicly traded, to the degree that they are judged suitable. While some of the principles may be more applicable to bigger organisations than to smaller businesses, regulators may aim to enhance awareness of good corporate governance. Individual market participants, board members, and firm leaders' business judgments are not to be influenced or second-guessed by the Principles.

What works in one firm or for one set of investors may not be relevant to all businesses or to issues of systemic economic significance. Employees' and other stakeholders' interests are recognised in the Principles, as well as their critical role in the company's long-term growth and performance. Other relevant factors toan organisation's decision-making processes, such as environmental, anti-corruption, or ethical concerns, are considered in the

Principles but are addressed more explicitly in a number of other instruments, such as the OECD Guidelines for Multinational Enterprises, the Convention on Combating Bribery of Foreign Public Officials in International Business Transactions, and the United Nations Convention on the Elimination of Racial Discrimination in International Business Transactions.

Other relevant factors to an organisation's decision-making processes, such as environmental, anti-corruption, or ethical concerns, are addressed more explicitly in a number of other instruments, such as the OECD Guidelines for Multinational Enterprises, the Convention on Combating Bribery of Foreign Public Officials in International Business Transactions, the UN Guiding Principles on Business and Human Rights, and the ILO Declaration on Fund Management.

"Corporate governance is concerned with holding the balance between economic and social goals and between individual and communal goals. The governance framework is there to encourage the efficient use of resources and equally to require accountability for the stewardship of those resources. The aim is to align as nearly as possible the interests of individuals, corporations and society." -Sir Adrian Cadbury, UK, Commission Report: Corporate Governance 1992.

The board's responsibilities are described in the OECD Principles of Corporate Governance (2004), and some of them are summarised below:

- Board members should be well-informed and act in the company's and shareholders' best interests by acting ethically and in good faith, with due diligence and care.

- Corporate strategy, goal-setting, key action plans, risk management, capital plans, and yearly budgets are all evaluated and directed in charge of overseeing significant purchases and divestitures.
- Key executives are chosen, compensated, monitored, and replaced, and succession planning is overseen.
- Align key executive and board remuneration (pay) with the company's and shareholders' long-term objectives.
- Ensure a proper and transparent nomination and election procedure for board members.
- Ensure the integrity of the company's accounting and financial reporting systems, as well as their independent auditing.
- Ascertain that adequate internal control systems are in place.
- Oversee the disclosure and communication processes.
- Where board committees are formed, their mandate, composition, and working processes should be clearly defined and made public.

Certain governance criteria must be met by companies listed on the New York Stock Exchange (NYSE) and other stock exchanges. The NYSE Listed Company Manual, for example, requires, among other things, Directors who are self-employed:

"A majority of independent Directors is required for listed businesses... In carrying out their tasks, effective boards of Directors use independent judgement. The need for a majority of independent Directors would improve board supervision and reduce the risk of serious conflicts of interest."

Section 303A.01 (Section 303A.01.) An independent Director is not employed by the firm and does not have a "material financial connection" with it. In order to enable non-management Directors to act as a more effective check on management, each listed company's non-management Directors must meet at regularly scheduled executive sessions without management.

Section 303A.03 (Section 303A.03). According to their charters, boards organise their members into committees with distinct functions. A nominating/corporate governance committee made up completely of independent Directors is required for publicly traded businesses. This committee is in charge of nominating new board members. Compensation and Audit Committees are also mentioned, with the latter subject to a number of listing rules as well as external restrictions. Keeping that concept in mind, the following are the basic components of good corporate governance:

The Board of Directors is responsible for a variety of responsibilities, including: Appointing and managing the Chief Executive Officer, as well as establishing a long-term strategic vision. A majority of independent Directors on the most effective boards are able to monitor corporate management and independent committees for the interests of shareholders. These Directors should be present at the meetings and ready to debate important topics. Long-serving Directors may get too enmeshed in their organisations to be regarded as fully independent. The habit of board members "overboarding" should likewise be a source of worry. This refers to circumstances in which Directors serve on the boards of too many different publicly listed organisations or nonprofit organisations to be successful.

As a result, these Directors may find themselves unable to attend meetings, prepare questions, address important problems, or provide proper service to the shareholders who elected them. Typically, the chairperson of the Board of Directors and the CEO ofan organisation should be appointed independently.

However, if there is an independent leadership position on the board, such as a lead Director to offer a counterweight, it may be suitable to combine the responsibilities. Otherwise, the combined CEO and chair may exert undue influence over the board, causing a conflict of interest. Allowing a CEO to create a loan with unsuitable or self-serving terms is an example of this sort of conflict.

How do you apply the corporate governance principles?

Corporate governance's central purpose is to increase long-term shareholder value while also safeguarding the interests of other stakeholders. Good corporate governance is essential not just for gaining credibility and trust, but also for survival, expansion, and consolidation as part of strategic management. Organisations that want to strengthen governance should examine their internal business structures, procedures, and initiatives closely. When it comes to determining what defines effective governance, the 10 principles listed below are a good place to start:

- Individual responsibilities, organisational expectations of leaders, and the functions of the executive and steering committees should all be clearly defined.
- An executive committee must be composed of the correct individuals, with special attention paid to each individual's background, talents, and experience, as well as how the addition of one person enhances the committee's collective potential and successful

functioning.

- The executive committee is responsible for establishing the organisation's vision, purpose, and strategy, as well as assisting the organisation in understanding them and adjusting plans to put them into action. Executive committees may assist in raising the possibility that their organisations will deliver on their goal by putting in place an effective system of risk supervision and internal controls.
- It is critical that the executive committee ensures that information flows to the board that aids decision-making; that there is transparency and accountability to external stakeholders and employees throughout the organisation; and that the integrity of financial statements and other key information is protected.
- The executive committee has a responsibility to play in improving the organisation's capacity and capabilities.
- The executive committee assistsan organisation in efficiently engaging with stakeholders and workers. Accountability entails taking responsibility for the strategy and tasks necessary to achieve organisational objectives. This applies to all levels of the organisation, from employees to senior executives, who embrace risk management within a formalised risk appetite. This includes cultivating a compliance culture in order to generate a real and perceived belief that the entity is operating within internal and external constraints.
- Treating all stakeholders, particularly minorities, fairly and equally, and providing appropriate remedies for infractions is what fairness entails. It is critical to establish efficient communication mechanisms in order to ensure the equitable and timely protection of resources and human assets, as well as the correction

of errors.The coexistence of state-owned, private, and international enterprises is a feature of our business sector. The composition of business boards, like the structure of ownership, has a significant impact on how organisations are governed and controlled. The Board of Directors is in charge of setting business goals, formulating broad policies, and appointing senior executives to carry out those goals and policies.

- Transparency means having nothing to conceal, allowing others to observe its procedures and transactions.Transparency is an important aspect of corporate governance since it guarantees that an outside observer may review all of an entity's actions at any time. In order to further transparency, non-direct actors must have trust that executive actors are directing the entity toward a pre-defined goal rather than using it for personal gain, as well as get expert advice on how the applied technique may be improved. Assurance services give objective, expert judgments that help to limit the danger of information leakage the risk that comes from incorrect information.
- Accountability is important. Defining and leading the organisation's objectives while adhering to the values and principles that govern how business is conducted.Those in charge of governance are in charge of these critical strategic concerns as well as providing leadership in developing the correct culture to drive the company's performance. The organisation will languish without clear direction, policy, and processes and is unlikely to achieve its long-term goals and potential. This should involve leadership and core expertise renewal to ensure knowledge and experience retention, as well as proper representation and continuity.

- Future-ready board members will have a profound sense of curiosity and a readiness to learn in order to achieve this. They'll be ready to adjust their perspective when they make a concerted attempt to listen to stakeholders who all have different and opposing expectations. They appreciate the interconnectedness of needs and are dedicated to creating solutions that satisfy environmental, stakeholder, and shareholder requirements. Future-ready stewards are collectively directed by a value-driven purpose that promotes health and well-being via proven action in resolving structural disparities in order to construct more equitable, diverse, and prepared businesses. A mission that extends beyond the goal and necessitates a high level of accountability in terms of keeping commitments.

Perhaps the Directors should have seen the problems earlier and adopted a different approach?

The structures and methods for the direction and management of businesses are referred to as corporate governance.It also involves the management, the Board of Directors, controlling shareholders, minority shareholders, and other stakeholders‘ interactions.

Openness to public disclosure, high transparency, and accountability are essential characteristics of good corporate governance that promote the long-term viability of businesses and society. Good corporate governance is required to avoid mismanagement by allowing organisations to function more effectively, enhance access to capital, limit risk, and protect stakeholders. It also makes businesses more responsible and transparent to investors, reducing the risk of expropriation and injustice to shareholders.

In order to prevent frequent boardroom prejudices, prospective board members should be able to not only express their own opinions but also actively engage with the perspectives of others. According to the poll results, a future-ready board member is honest and specific in their questions and is wary of accepting answers at face value.

Board members should also be truthful in their efforts to bring all aspects of diversity to the table, as well as a perspective that may not have existed previously. Each board position must be filled by someone who has a global citizen attitude and is dedicated to taking steps to improve diversity, equity, and inclusion.

"I am not bound to win, but I am bound to be true. I am not bound to succeed, but I am bound to live by the light that I have. I must stand with anybody that stands right, and stand with him while he is right, and part with him when he goes wrong." – Abraham Lincoln

According to studies, companies with more varied boards of Directors are more risk averse, have less volatile stock returns, and are more likely to pay dividends. As a result, it may be argued that a primary aim for the makeup of any company's board and senior management ranks should be diversity by gender, age, and minority participation.

The evaluation and monitoring of remuneration at both the board and top management levels is another important aspect of corporate governance. Typically, the chairperson of the Board of Directors and the CEO of an organisation should be appointed independently. However, if there is an independent leadership position on the board, such as a lead Director to offer a counterweight, it may be suitable to combine the responsibilities.

Otherwise, the combined CEO and chair may exert undue influence over the board, causing a conflict of interest. Allowing a CEO to create a loan with unsuitable or self-serving terms is an example of this sort of conflict. Pay should be linked to performance, with a focus on long-term goals. By avoiding guaranteed compensation and expensive severance packages, you may avoid "paying for failure." For effective supervision, establish an independent pay committee. Ensure that compensation disclosures are transparent and complete. Pay non-executive Directors and keep track of their compensation. Nonexecutive Directors who are overpaid may not be able to make impartial decisions about managers' pay and performance.

A study of auditing methods and financial reporting might potentially flag impending concerns. Auditors should be impartial (with no financial stake in a corporation) and make the majority of their money from auditing rather than consulting.

Accounting difficulties should be handled in a transparent manner, with comprehensive, thorough information and reports available to the board at all times, and safeguards in place to avoid a recurrence of any dubious findings. Auditing strengthens the trustworthiness of any company's financial reporting. The auditing process guarantees that financial accounts are accurate and full, making them more reliable and valuable for investment choices. Along with the idea that ownership structure matters in corporate governance, there's also the idea that the company's financial structure, or the ratio of debt to equity, has an impact on governance quality.

The level of corporate governance is largely determined by the legal, regulatory, and political context in which an organisation works. Corporate governance processes are, in reality, economic and legal entities that are frequently the result of political decisions. For example, the extent to which shareholders can exert control over management is determined by their voting rights as defined by company law, and the extent to which creditors can exercise financial claims against a bankrupt unit is determined by bankruptcy laws and procedures, among other factors.

Shareholder rights should also be considered a vital component of effective governance by investors. Multiple shares/classes are not always indicative of weak governance, but they are something to think about. For example, in the information technology industry, it is customary for firm founders and insiders to own shares with more voting rights than outside investors.

- Is it possible for shareholders to put suggestions on proxy ballots or nominate Directors?
- What activities, such as modifying the company's bylaws, may a board conduct without shareholder approval?
- Are there any measures in place to make it difficult foran organisation to be bought, such as poison pills?
- How is management compensated in the case of a takeover?

Shareholder recognition, which is a policy that guarantees that all shareholders have a vote inan organisation's inner workings, is one of the principles of corporate governance. The value of an organisation's shares is also secured by shareholder recognition. To ensure that everyone has the same vision of the company's future, the rules and duties of board members must be clearly defined. Stakeholder interest is concerned with the needs of those who are not stockholders. As a result of reaching out to non-members, greater communication and ties with the press and the community are fostered. Corporate governance ethical rules are also critical for ensuring increased profits and keeping the organisation out of legal difficulties. Employees and board members are also subject to these restrictions. Transparency must be visible, and it should be.

Investors are increasingly using proxy voting to impact a board's corporate supervision and commitment to improving governance on problems including climate change, income inequality, and shareholder proxy access. Shareholders must be able to send a message to the Board of Directors by withholding votes for Directors if the firm has failed to act on winning shareholder motions, failed to deal with a Director's poor performance, or failed to strengthen board accountability and supervision. Those in charge of governance should identify important stakeholders and how they interact with the business, as well as how they are engaged, in order to secure the best possible outcome for the company. The yearly agenda and strategy plan incorporate stakeholder interaction.

Is there any role of Ethics and Compliance in corporate culture?

Corporate culture is defined as a mix of the beliefs, attitudes, and behaviours expressed by a corporation in its operations and relationships with its stakeholders. While corporate governance regulations and standards have improved compliance and the adoption of best practises, they have had far less success in transforming business cultures. Despite considerable reform initiatives and improved knowledge of corporate governance over the last two decades or more, governance failures appear to be on the rise.

Given their linked meanings, consider how ethics and compliance play a critical role in fostering a strong business culture. When discussing businesses doing the right thing, the phrases "ethics" and "compliance" are sometimes used interchangeably. While they both seek to attain comparable objectives, they are not the same thing. If you want to improve your corporate culture, you need to first comprehend the link between the two as well as the small differences that distinguish them. There are certain distinctions to be made between the words "ethics" and "compliance." They are certainly linked, but they are not the same thing. Take a look at these ethical and compliance definitions for further information.

According to the Ethics and Compliance Initiative, ethics is "the judgments, choices, and acts (behaviours) we make that reflect and execute our beliefs." A set of behaviour norms that govern decisions and actions based on responsibilities drawn from fundamental principles. Conforming or adjusting one's activities to the wishes of another, a rule, or necessity is referred to as compliance. So, while you may be following compliance criteria, your reason may be to stay within the law rather than because you believe it is ethically correct. To put it simply, consider how a youngster behaves when no one is looking. Is he afraid of getting caught by the store manager or screamed at by his parents if he steals a candy bar (compliance with rules and expectations)? Or does he just refrain from stealing because he understands it is bad to take anything that is not his (directed by an internal moral compass)? Ethics, on the other hand, takes a proactive approach, guiding you to moral thought and action based on your own internal motivations of character, values, and ideals.

Compliance, on the other hand, takes a more reactive approach, requiring you to make a deliberate decision to follow a rule or piece of legislation that someone else made. Given their linked meanings, consider how ethics and compliance play a critical role in fostering a strong business culture.

What are the benefits of ethics impacting corporate culture if you are more interested in establishing a good culture than avoiding a poor one (bad ethics equal a bad culture)?

Employees like to work for a boss they can rely on. Employees want to feel protected, secure, appreciated, and respected. That is something we all want. Fostering an ethical compliance culture increases all of these aspects of a pleasant, thriving company environment, hence improving employee morale. When you create a code of conduct that sets expectations for fair treatment and ethical behaviour, you provide workers with the guidelines they need to behave professionally. This written code frequently goes above and beyond what the law demands, and it serves as a solid basis for fostering a culture of respect, trust, openness, and responsibility.

According to research, "upholding ethical principles in the workplaces improves office manager performance," especially when the code of conduct coincides with employees' own beliefs." Increases compliance. While an action or conduct is legally permissible, it is not always ethical. The foundation of legal compliance is an emphasis on corporate ethics. Both are required to establish and maintain an ethical compliance culture. The more you express your beliefs and principles, give training to match them, and hold every person responsible, the less risky and more compliant you will be.

Cultural transformation begins with fresh messaging. Culture-changing communication is nonverbal—the "doing" rather than the "saying"—and is most visibly manifested via leadership actions. People modify their conduct when they realise there are new standards for membership. A little adjustment in the conduct of a top manager may send a powerful message.

In other words, how do you promote business ethics and develop a corporate compliance culture?

Write down your expectations. This must be done in the form of an official, trackable policy; otherwise, your ethics and compliance initiatives would be toothless. After you've completed the initial stage of developing written policies, you'll need someone to supervise your company's ethical and compliance activities. This improves the efficiency of your overall ethical and compliance procedures. What is the secret to a successful compliance program? Putting a corporate compliance officer (CCO) in charge as opposed to a figurehead with no actual power In this role, the CCO is a champion of corporate integrity, ethics, and responsibility, which are the foundations of a compliance culture.

"To alter a culture, leaders must alter the signals that individuals get about what they must do to fit in."

To begin, you'll need a comprehensive policy document, especially a written code of conduct and/or code of ethics policy. Employees must be aware that they may consult a reference to learn what the company expects of them. Setting uniform expectations and holding all employees accountable to meet standards is the essence of accountability in your firm. You may create an ethical compliance culture by clearly defining the company's purpose, values, and objectives and implementing regulations such as a written code of conduct to match the vision, values, and goals.

Emphasising the significance of accountability in your organisation will help foster a proactive culture of responsibility among employees at all levels, from part-time hourly workers to C-suite executives. Building trust, improving performance, strengthening company culture, increasing morale, and increasing compliance are all benefits of promoting organisational responsibility. The basic line is that you must examine how individuals are performing in comparison to what is expected.

"Leaders' behaviour shows what individuals with power—and those who desire to acquire it—are expected to do."

The next stage is to inform your employees about your ethical and compliance initiatives thus far. You might approach this in a variety of ways, including one-on-one and small group meetings, bulk email distribution, and phone conferences. Whatever communication tools you choose, the aim is to communicate your ethical principles clearly and consistently and to ensure that workers understand how these policies affect their duties. Workplace communication may be challenging, especially when conveying intangible "ethical culture" signals. However, by creating a safe environment for communication, establishing clear standards (in terms of channel, frequency, and expectations), and doing so regularly, you increase your chances of successful top-down, bottom up, side-to-side collaboration throughout your organisation.

Just because you design a code of ethics policy, establish standards, and explain it to workers does not always imply they understand it. This is where the training comes into play. It is critical that you train in accordance with your ethical policies. Training must be meaningful, just as "book learning" is not the same as "hands-on application of information." Sharing the policy with employees and explaining the whys and hows of ethics and compliance establishes a solid foundation of understanding.

However, teaching employees how each policy aspect explicitly pertains to the day-to-day duties they perform offers the needed real-world link. Furthermore, covering a topic on a frequent basis in training emphasises its crucial relevance. Conversations and training regarding ethics and compliance reinforce the fact that your firm takes them both seriously. Furthermore, the more you talk about ethics and compliance and teach employees about the regulations that govern them, the better equipped they will be to behave in certain scenarios.

Is it true that ethics and compliance are important in business?

Our first stop on our market research journey was introspection, looking at our own experiences as employees and employers. We tracked the situations in which we saw loyalty, and we realised that, in the eyes of the beholder, loyalty is evident when it exists, crystal clear when it does not, but it is also practically hard to define when it rests in the grey region. Unfortunately, the majority of people fall within the grey region. So, how do we define loyalty? Is it a fiction of our mind, an ethereal sensation, or an objectively anchored product of something? For us, loyalty is influenced by three factors: the leader's vision, the entire environment in which we operate, and organisational culture. Having said that, we know that loyalty is difficult to measure when workforces contain a variety of generations—baby boomers, Gen Z, and Gen

Y—all coexisting, each with a unique perspective and loyalty metric. Furthermore, today's workplace is different; it no longer relates to a physical office where upward mobility is as visible as the C-suite on the top floor. It is cloud-based, networked, social, mobile, and global, with employees who may be contingent workers, consultants, or even gig workers. A one-size-fits-all approach to loyalty will not work in this day and age.

If you actually want to change your company's culture, your ethics and compliance activities should not be one-and-done. It's not going to happen with a simple letter or written instruction. Most importantly, your reason for change should be about more than just protecting your bases or avoiding liability. It must stem from your desire to foster a healthy ethical and compliance culture that is consistent with your company's purpose, vision, and values. To accomplish meaningful, long-term change, begin with your "why."

"It makes no difference if they remain for two or three years; what counts is how strongly they feel about the organisation while they are there."

So, what can a corporation do to flourish ethically? Instead than concentrating on the bad choices you want your workers to avoid, concentrate on the good ones. Rather of gathering top management to create a "values statement," business executives can instead facilitate a series of organised talks between leaders at all levels and their teams. The purpose of these discussions should be to create a common vocabulary that can be used to construct instances of how people live out the organisation's principles or classical virtues. This is an intrinsically social process - virtue is acquired rather than inherited. Leaders are already instructors of their culture, whether they realise it or not, and should consider how they may do it more effectively. Here are questions that businesses may use to frame these dialogues and change their focus away from compliance and toward ethical excellence.

- When has trust made us more nimble and faster?
- How can we rebuild trust?
- How do we gain and deepen trust at our best?
- How does compassion help us achieve our corporate objectives?
- How does compassion improve participation?
- When have acts of kindness aided our business results?
- When have you seen courage in our organisation?
- Who is effective in inspiring others to be courageous?
- How can we encourage individuals to be braver?
- When have we gone out of our way as a corporation to assist a coworker?
- How can we further empower our people so that they are more involved in making their own decisions?
- When have we done our utmost to meet the demands of all of our stakeholders?
- What were our wisest decisions?
- When faced with the most difficult decisions, when did we select the better path and have the fortitude to persevere?
- How can we be more deliberate in incorporating wisdom into decision-making?
- How can we reconcile two opposing rights, such as concern for the firm versus care for the person or compassion versus justice?
- How can we assist folks in developing self-control?

- When have we done the best job of supporting life-work balance?
- What aspects of working for our firm do you appreciate the most?
- What aspects of working for our firm do you appreciate the most?
- What do we do well, and how could we do it better?
- When was our culture at its pinnacle?
- How successfully do we instil character in our employees?
- How can character development help our company?
- What steps are being taken to foster or inhibit character development in our organisation?
- How can character development help lower risk?
- How does character development contribute to growth?

The objective is not perfection; organisations are neither entirely virtuous nor entirely devoid of virtue. The objective is for businesses to be better than they were before and for executives to lead by example. We believe it is vital for an organisation to ensure that stories about the practise of virtue are actively and purposefully communicated throughout the organisation. Daily acts—planning meetings, quarterly reports, RFPs, customer encounters, and so on—shape character.

"We are what we continually do," Aristotle.

Thus, excellence is a habit, not an act. In turn, virtues pervade company culture and determine "how things are done around here." That is a much more powerful force than a narrow emphasis on obeying the rules. History often appears to repeat itself. In most other nations across the world where there is concentrated ownership, independent Directors are often appointed by controlling shareholders and are often accountable to these shareholders. Not unexpectedly, they have frequently failed to play a role in questioning choices that are not always in the company's or all shareholders' best interests. According to me, the notion of independent Directors may fall out of favour and cease to be a credible instrument for guaranteeing effective corporate governance.

In reality, in many nations, severe reservations about the usefulness of independent Directors have already been airborne. As we've previously mentioned, the formation of corporate regulation is frequently tied to perceived failures of organisations and their management to perform as society expects. This trend is not unique to corporate governance, and, like with accounting, various nations may face challenges at different periods. Some of the most well remembered examples of corporate governance failure are addressed.

"Organisations need to practice qualitative corporate governance rather than quantitative governance thereby ensuring it is properly run." – and "You cannot legislate good behaviour." – Mervyn King

In 2022, 136 organisations are recognised for their unwavering commitment to business integrity. The honorees span 22 countries and 45 industries, and include 14 first-time honorees and 6 organisations that have been named to the honoree list 16 times, marking every year since its inception.

1. 3M (Industrial Manufacturing) United States
2. Accenture (Consulting Services) Ireland
3. ADM (Food, Beverage & Agriculture) United States
4. AECOM (Engineering Services) United States
5. Alfac Incor. (Accident & Life Insurance) United States
6. Allianz Life (Accident & Life Insurance) United States

7. Apple (Technology) United States
8. Aptiv PLC (Automotive) Ireland
9. ARM Semiconductors United Kingdom
10. AT&T (Telecomm) United States
11. Avangrid (Energy & Utilities) United States
12. Avista (Energy & Utilities) United States
13. Baptist (Health Healthcare Providers) United States
14. Best Buy Co. (Retail) United states
15. Blue Shield Health (insurance) California
16. BMO Fin Gr. (Banks) Canada
17. Booz Allen Hamilton (Consultation) United States
18. Brown- Forman (Food- Beverage) United States
19. Cambia Health (Health Insurance) United States
20. Canon U.S.A (Imaging Technology) United States
21. Capgemini (Consultation) France
22. Capital Power (Energy & Utilities) Canada
23. Carefirst Health (Insurance) United States
24. CBRE (Real States) United States
25. Cementos Argos (Construction) Colombia

"Corporate governance is the system by which companies are directed and controlled. It encompasses the entire mechanics of the functioning ofan organisation and attempt to put in place a system of checks and balances between the shareholders, Directors, employees, auditor and the management." Cadbury Committee (U.K.), 1992

Starbucks COO Rosalind Brewer Rosalind Brewer belongs to a modern leadership school that thinks that leadership is an issue of privilege. Rosalind, the CEO of Starbucks and former CEO of Sam's Club, believes in the value of ethical leadership. She believes in a six-point leadership style that emphasises honesty, candour, and respect. Rosalind feels that these elements of leadership contribute significantly to the development of strong teams and exceptional businesses. It fosters a culture of trust within organisations, where bosses are no longer viewed as the enemy, but rather as a fellow partner with common aims.

Don't ask your parents to do anything you're not willing to do. Our workplaces are social microcosms. Virtue is required to protect civilizations and communities from crumbling as a result of ruthless personal or professional objectives. The same is true in the workplace. When the wrong thing promises quick gain, it requires courage and endurance to do the right thing. However, as numerous business leaders throughout history have demonstrated over and again, honesty is what builds successful enterprises.

Good governance means that your company's operations are designed to produce outcomes that fulfil societal and organisational needs while making smart use of its resources. Because strong leadership is needed to drive inspiration within an organisation, these policies and principles are first practised and influenced by leadership. This is a crucial component of success since it allows for the establishment of growth prospects and a competitive edge. For organisations to position themselves favourably in order to weather a challenging economic climate, good corporate governance has become a crucial emphasis area.

Recurring reviews are an important part of effective governance. Sub-committees must assess performance in order to determine if project, process, system, departmental, or data improvements have met their objectives. They will be required to offer improvements or ideas that would enhance procedures and systems in many circumstances. The Executive Committee can then evaluate these recommendations to see if they want to support these courses and spend money on them, or if they want to develop other plans or objectives for progress. If the organisation's strategic plan has to be updated, the Executive Committee is the one who makes the modifications.

Few people have Azim Premji's sense for profitable, long-term enterprises. He was exclusively responsible for transforming a family-run FMCG company into an FMCG and IT powerhouse. At the same time, Mr. Premji believes in paying it forward through the Azim Premji Foundation and University, which are both socially engaged and involved. He has established a stellar reputation as an employer and corporate citizen for both himself and his company. His personal commitment to ethics has played a part in his extraordinary accomplishments. All of this contributes to Wipro's reputation as one of the most ethical organisations in the world, not just in India. Wipro was named the most ethical company in a list prepared by the Ethisphere Institute.

"The true threat toan organisation comes from within, from low ethical standards and a lack of integrity, which can do irreparable harm."- Azim Premji

History has consistently demonstrated that business ethics, shared values, and corporate governance affect an enterprise's longevity. What is necessary is "capacity building" in order to engage in more ethical behavior. Employees must understand that compliance is more than a checkbox exercise, and they must see their organisations go beyond compliance and incorporate ethical standards into daily operations. They must be empowered to prevent unethical behaviour at work and recognise that corporate integrity is directly tied to the future of the firm, their families, and their lives.

Chief compliance officers (CCOs) have identified compliance culture as one of their top concerns for almost a decade. As a result, actions to build corporate culture have been prioritised. Despite increased money and attention, companies have had little long-term success in developing a vibrant culture of ethics and integrity.

"Knowing the wrong thing to do does not always imply doing the right thing."

Most organisations' attempts to enhance culture begin at the top, with senior leaders demonstrating high ethics in their interactions and communications with their workers. However, these initiatives frequently fail to detect the most powerful source of impact on employees' perceptions of culture and ethical actions: their peers.

According to the Gartner Compliance and Ethics Global Culture Assessment, a top-down strategy has a minor impact on culture. CCOs, on the other hand, may significantly enhance their culture by concentrating on creating and fostering a favourable atmosphere within the organisation. Compliance is more important than ever. Compliance has long been a problem that affects businesses, but recent events such as the global financial crisis have focused attention on governance in the financial industry.

Organisations across the board are under increasing pressure to increase openness and responsibility for compliance. According to Thomson Reuters' Cost of Compliance Report, 74% of compliance professionals globally expect that the emphasis on controlling regulatory risk will rise over the next year.

Following the implementation of the Senior Managers and Certification Regime (SMCR) in the financial services industry, compliance officers are now concerned about personal liability.It was first adopted in the banking industry in 2016, then the insurance sector in December 2018, and finally all financial sector organisations by the end of 2019. As a result, according to Thomson Reuters research, 54% of compliance experts expect personal responsibility to climb in the next 12 months. Senior managers may be found guilty of misconduct under SMCR if a regulatory breach occurs in their area of responsibility and they are unable to present proof of having taken reasonable efforts to prevent it.

According to Gartner research, the major distinction between good and poor corporate cultures is climate, which refers to the practises and procedures that workers follow as well as the signals they get about which behaviours are rewarded and appreciated. A positive atmosphere is associated with higher compliance and overall firm success. When asked, over 75% of employees recognised themselves as working in businesses with poor climates. To make matters worse, only one-quarter of employees believe their colleagues engage in and model ethical behavior.

"Your business will not have a positive atmosphere if employees just know how to prevent wrongdoing."

This is crucial: organisations with strong cultures beat companies with weaker cultures in terms of both financial and nonfinancial goals. In powerful cultures: provide detailed examples that allow each employee to learn how to show these behaviours in their everyday workflows to help employees understand what excellent conduct looks like. Your organisation will not have a positive atmosphere if employees simply know how to prevent wrongdoing.

Employees are 90% less likely to witness wrongdoing. Employees who see wrongdoing are 1.5 times more likely to report it. Employees are more than twice as likely to be involved with their job and organisation and nearly 2.5 times more likely to put in extra effort. Efforts to build a compliance culture of integrity fail to provide long-term business results in the absence of a robust atmosphere.

Though effective Ethics & Compliance programmes may not be the first thing that comes to mind for a non-compliance officer when describing a successful organisation, ethics and compliance genuinely create the framework for long-term success. For example, compliance training and an introduction toan organisation's code of conduct are frequently a new employee's first glimpse into corporate culture, establishing organisational values and setting the tone from the start. While continuing education is necessary to maintain regulatory compliance, it also functions as a cultural touchpoint for current workers.

Organisations now have the chance to identify and pursue their mission, whether that is through the product or service supplied or through the internal philosophy of how workers are treated (or both!). One method to assure long-term operations and growth, as well as a culture that attracts and maintains great employees, is to do it with ethics and compliance in mind.

A weak corporate culture, on the other hand, results in a restricted pipeline of top talent and a lack of compliance with company rules, laws and regulations, and social conventions, which raises total business risk. However, just 12% of organisations believe they are fostering the "correct culture," which supports communication, inclusion, frequent training, and strong business principles.

Organisations who exhibited visionary leadership and a comprehensive approach to risk and compliance management These companies have developed and implemented a coordinated, enterprise-wide programme that addresses many risk categories such as internal reporting, third-party risk management, employees training, ESG, and others.

I admire them for their efforts in repairing their reputation and developing a successful programme focusing on actions that match their principles. They rehabilitated their company culture, procedures, and governance through a people-centric strategy that emphasised organisational trust, exhibiting genuine resiliency and exceptional adherence to proactive ethics, compliance, and risk management.

They efficiently recognised reporting trends and kept their board updated along the process. They also used specialised training to educate their large workforce base on compliance issues including data privacy, competition law, and anti-corruption. They were able to use risk rate to accelerate third-party approval procedures and develop workflows across their field, procurement, and legal teams.

A weak corporate culture, on the other hand, results in a restricted pipeline of top talent and a lack of compliance with company rules, laws, and regulations, as well as social conventions, which raises total business risk. However, just 12% of organisations believe they are fostering the "correct culture," which supports communication, inclusion, frequent training, and strong business principles.

As a result, corporate culture is a good indicator of the quality ofan organisation's risk and compliance program. Lower risk and higher compliance will inevitably follow if some aspects of culture (such as ethics) improve. To be successful in this evolution, organisations must carefully cultivate the type of corporate culture that breeds compliance. Here are few high-value strategies for starting to build a positive culture that reduces risk and aids in compliance:

- Leaders must identify which elements of their corporate culture are most important to them and then ensure that these elements are implemented and practised throughout the organisation. This is a logical first step since it establishes the basis for what makes a culture strong: its values. When these principles are openly communicated and broadly understood inside the organisation, they drive the anticipated actions. For example, if acting with integrity is a core value, employees must understand what that entails as well as which actions are rewarded and which are not.
- Training is also important for supporting corporate principles since it provides employees with the information they need to act. To limit liability concerns, I advocate training that includes not just rules and regulations but also corporate principles, both during onboarding and during workers‘ stays at the business. When training is done thoroughly, it creates a healthy workplace culture and may frequently alleviate any problems before they develop. It is in the best interests of an organisation for HR and compliance to work together, as both are crucial to creating a compliant, safe, and inclusive workplace.
- Many aspects contribute to an organisation's success, but staying on top of ethics and compliance is one of the most important. Ethics and compliance should be a top focus for any in-house lawyer, compliance and ethics officer, human resources executive, outside counsel, or risk management consultant. In an increasingly stringent regulatory climate, it is critical to put in place

an effective compliance programme right away. Your programme should emphasise enhanced accountability and openness, among other things.

- Creating a strong speak-up culture in which workers feel empowered—and comfortable—speaking out against wrongdoing can also help to strengthen business culture. The most effective speak-up programmes are those that are transparent, do not allow for impunity, and encourage workers to speak out internally against misconduct.

While having an ethical culture on paper makesan organisation compliant, businesses must think broader and build an atmosphere in which they behave with integrity because they want to be compliant (not just because they need to). There is a significant difference between these incentives, and it is felt by employees throughout the organisation. Take, for example, diversity programmes. Last year, the United States The Securities and Exchange Commission (SEC) has adopted a new Nasdaq Stock Exchange listing rule. It requires all Nasdaq-listed corporations to have at least two diverse directors on their boards. This is one of the first formal listing regulations that requires organisations to prioritise diversity, and it has since been a catalyst for organisations to reconsider their corporate culture. Organisations, on the other hand, should not hire more diverse people simply because the law compels them to do so.

Companies like McKinsey have well-researched and documented that "the most diverse companies are now more likely than ever to outperform less diverse peers on profitability." From a cultural standpoint, Catalyst, a nonprofit whose goal is to build workplaces that work for women, finds that diversity and inclusion have been shown to improve employee recruitment and retention, grow innovation, and reduce groupthink, among other benefits.

In conclusion, the responsibility that an individual assumes when charged with the governance of an entity is significant, and it should only be undertaken with a clear understanding of, and commitment to, fulfilling this responsibility to the best of their ability, first and foremost for the benefit of the stakeholders. Individual and organisational performance will both benefit froman organisation grasp of the concepts and practises of good governance, so how do you and your company do against this checklist? Organisations can benefit from good governance in a variety of ways, including strategies and plans that are better; efficiencies and effectiveness of operations and processes have improved; project management and delivery have improved; compliance with regulatory requirements, as well as financial and risk management, has become more conservative; improved communication and engagement among members and stakeholders/employees; enhanced agility with which an organisation can carry out its mission and objectives.

This is where HR and compliance teams may collaborate, as compliance teams must educate the company on the benefits of a more diverse workforce (while also complying with applicable regulations) and HR teams must help source talent. And, as with any other risk and compliance programme, reporting metrics and standards must be in place so that organisations can determine whether they are successfully moving the needle on their cultural objectives, which will influence progress toward mandated compliance targets.

Finally, and probably most crucially, a healthy corporate culture isan organisation-wide endeavour, which means that leadership teams and board members must set a good example. Often, HR is blamed for workplace culture, and while HR is helpful, they are not the only ones that define it. Indeed, good corporate culture must be the result of a C-Suite debate in which executives identify what the firm stands for and the sort of atmosphere they want to establish.

Organisations will discover that when executive teams set the tone for a strong culture, it translates into long-term value generation and risk reduction. Leaders, for example, should be courteous and considerate to employees during meetings to demonstrate the type of professional behaviour that is anticipated. This might range from demonstrating genuine interest in team successes and milestones to soliciting employee feedback on current and future company operations. Providing this degree of respect and openness fosters an atmosphere in which workers follow suit in their respective roles and duties, which helps to prevent negative conduct and possible risk in the long term.

There are several advantages to improving company culture that go beyond simply making the workplace a more enjoyable and collaborative setting. While both are crucial, a strong culture built in shared and acted upon business principles will find organisations decreasing risk, boosting compliance, and, most significantly, establishing a business that attracts excellent talent, customers, partners, and other critical stakeholders. Enable small teams and groups of employees to collaborate on beneficial ethical actions.

The tendency toward personal accountability makes it even more critical for organisations to be completely compliant. The greatest risk to achieving and maintaining compliance inan organisation is its employees. Expertly crafted rules and processes, as well as well-considered controls, are all meaningless if your employees do not comprehend or comply with them.

Noncompliance can take the form of both inadvertent and purposeful actions. Employees not understanding the necessity of compliance or how the regulations relate to their work are risk factors on the unintended side. Compliance problems can also be caused by confusing, erroneous, or ineffective communications from the top, as well as by inadequate training.

Obtaining 100% compliance is a massive burden and an obligation for every business. It is hard to completely eliminate noncompliance, especially if an individual chooses to take actions on purpose. It is critical to train employees and ensure that they understand their obligations, the company's expectations, and the penalties of noncompliance.

Mitigating the risk of unintended noncompliance is one step toward compliance that a business can take since it is within its control. This role is being made much easier by technological solutions that simplify both compliance training and monitoring. Learning management systems (LMS) make it possible to provide focused, engaging, and up-to-date compliance training. They provide easy access to data and reports to those who are ultimately accountable for keeping track of who has completed and, more importantly, who has not completed training.

How to establish a compliance and conscientious culture?

It is critical for the compliance function to lead the way in training selection, not only because they have the requisite skills to judge the quality of the content but also because they will be held personally responsible for noncompliance. Furthermore, if they have no say in picking the training, they may be dissatisfied with it. And how can we expect our students to be delighted if they aren't?

Aside from making the information more relevant, there are additional methods to make training more interesting. According to research, using a variety of training modalities engages audiences and has a beneficial impact on an organisation's risk profile. Short videos and apps make it simple to access material at any time and from any location, lowering the obstacles to training completion. Giving individuals a choice might sometimes be enough to make a difference. While some employees prefer desktop learning, where they can finish training at their workstation, others choose mobile learning, where they can study when and where they want. We all learn in unique ways. By expanding the possibilities, we give people the opportunity to study in a way that is more suitable for them. The goal of compliance training is to modify people's behaviour, knowledge, or both, and training programmes should be evaluated on this basis.

How can you persuade people to comply?

You cannot repeat the same teachings year after year; that is not training but rather awareness-raising. Training should be updated to make it more diverse and entertaining. Using a recent occurrence that is relevant to your company's industry to illustrate a point might be enough to make it feel contemporary. Employees want concrete examples that demonstrate what their own obligations are. It is not their responsibility to be familiar with every law or standard of conduct. It is critical that the training be applicable to the position. When people realise how it pertains to their profession, they will naturally get interested.

Employees want concrete examples that demonstrate what their own obligations are. It is not their responsibility to be familiar with every law or standard of conduct. It is critical that the training be applicable to the position. This is where technological compliance training solutions come in handy. Companies may build customised training content that is completely tailored to their needs. This includes utilising the organisation's name, the names of its policies, the language it employs, and even the names of specific individuals inside the corporation.

Many compliance professionals face the difficulty of not being assigned the personal responsibility of selecting training courses. It is the responsibility of HR or procurement to choose and select a training provider under the learning and development (L&D) mandate. The issue is that neither HR nor procurement have the necessary subject-area knowledge to make an educated conclusion. From the standpoint of HR L&D, it may be tempting to go for the "bells and whistles" option, which includes a plethora of movies, games, and other interactive components. And procurement may be primarily concerned with cost. However, the quality of the information will ultimately determine engagement.

The most difficult aspect of engaging employees in compliance training is that compliance is not their job. As humans, we focus our efforts on what we are assessed for and compensated for. For example, if you work at a retail bank, your job performance will be assessed by your day-to-day task efficiency and the degree of client service you provide. Your compensation will most likely be determined by how well you perform in customer satisfaction surveys.

And it is in these areas that you will concentrate your efforts. Making the curriculum relevant to their position is the key to engaging employees with compliance training. Otherwise, people won't be interested, and why would they be if they don't understand how it pertains to them?

"Learning is difficult, but forgetting is simple. The true measure of every learning programme is how effectively individuals retain what they have learned."

In fact, inadequate training might result in inadvertent noncompliance. As we stated in the last section, the degree to which the subjects are personalised to the specific individual and deliver meaningful benefits will determine whether employees retain the knowledge they learn from the training. If you can't convince your employees that compliance is vital to them, their customers, the firm, and the industry, it won't become part of your daily business culture. Banking employees, for example, must be trained not just how to avoid money laundering but also why it is necessary. Get them to understand that money laundering is more than simply the domain of drug lords and corrupt dictators; it also fuels and perpetuates global crime, deprives governments of tax income, and undermines our industry's legitimacy. Communicating to workers that their duty is to assist the company in preventing this and that the training is meant to assist them in understanding how they may assist the company in achieving that aim becomes an empowering statement. You'll have their entire attention if you can convince them to think about their joint role in the cause.

Making compliance management more efficient is another challenge. The compliance officer's job does not end with conducting training sessions. They must constantly check employees' development and the effectiveness of their training programmes. They must also be on the lookout for'red ags,' or those who may pose a threat.

According to a Deloitte and Compliance Week poll, the most popular technique to evaluate compliance training is to see how many employees finish it.However, monitoring completion rates tells us nothing about the quality of training or its effectiveness - that is, how much people actually learn and apply. You can go before the Board and state that 95% of workers completed the training course in the first month it was available and scored between 80% and 100%, but this tells us nothing about how compliant your company is.

Compliance officers must often prepare reports, and an LMS may help save time by giving access to data with the press of a button. What compliance officers truly want is assurance that people who have undergone the training understand what they are doing. As a result, several training courses include confidence buttons. If the compliance officer notices that a person got an answer wrong but was adamant that they got it correctly, this definitely indicates a problem.

There is also disagreement over how close the training and assessment should be. If the evaluation is administered immediately following the training, you may be testing people's recollection rather than their capacity to learn and comprehend compliance. However, if the questions are posed six months after the training programme and answered properly, you may be confident that the employees' knowledge has been successfully ingrained and the training has been effective.

Compliance is becoming easier to assess thanks to technological solutions such as LMSs. According to PwC's

State of Compliance research, 66% of compliance officers use technology to monitor workers' policy compliance. This all comes back to the significance of selecting the proper training programme by the right people. If the supplier is not chosen by the compliance department, you will not engage employees and will not establish a compliance culture since the individuals selecting the material do not understand the significance of it.

Other tools and paperwork that address employees inquiries and jog memory about certain procedures can also aid in compliance. Mobile app development is becoming more popular in the dissemination of compliance content, making it easier for employees to access real-time information.solutions to any rules queries they may have these tools may be especially valuable for new legislation, such as the General Data Protection Regulation (GDPR), when individuals learn what they imply for them in their employment.

Measuring how long it takes people to finish the training can also give helpful information. If someone moves really swiftly, you could wonder how much attention they were paying. Similarly, if someone takes an unusually lengthy time to finish a task, this may indicate that they difficulty with the subject. Both situations might be considered red flags for noncompliance. Both situations might be considered red flags for noncompliance. It's also helpful to observe which questions or areas people are struggling with. This might suggest a flaw in the training programme that needs to be addressed, and it could even lead the compliance function to conduct a face-to-face training session on that specific topic.

When it comes to reporting, organisations everywhere are under pressure to provide complete transparency around compliance, whether to fulfil government requirements or industry standards or to retain qualifications and certifications. Compliance officers must often prepare reports, and an LMS may help save time by giving access to data with the press of a button. However, as we've shown throughout this section, in order for an organisation to genuinely demonstrate compliance, an LMS must provide more than simply a list of courses with checkboxes next to each employee's name. The risk environment is always changing, and organisations must adapt to shifting compliance requirements. We are in the midst of a transition in terms of governance, risk management, and compliance (GRC).

Many countries are plagued by political insecurity. The Brexit discussions in the United Kingdom are nearing their conclusion, but we are still no closer to knowing what they will imply from a regulatory standpoint. Then there's the proposed SMCR expansion, which will affect the most senior management of regulated organisations. A specific training package on the subject may enough for many, but for those who wish to go further into important ideas or focus on certain jobs, a bespoke programme may be more suited. Companies, like the GDPR, must be prepared to engage in effective training programmes to ensure their employees has the necessary knowledge and awareness to comply with the new standards.

Has the organisation's policy and procedure been incorporated, including via frequent training?

As new training requirements and priorities arise, rms must be prepared with suitable training programmes to bring its sta up to speed. Of course, we should not simply update our training materials as new GRC concerns emerge. If the organisation's policy changes, the training content must be evaluated and updated. Some businesses also use compliance monitoring data to adjust their training programmes. Then there are general modifications that must be made to keep the training relevant year after year. The PwC State of Compliance research found that 49% of organisations annually update their compliance training and communication programmes. Digital systems are significantly easier to update than manual training programmes, and the on-demand feature of an LMS ensures that everyone has instant access to the most up-to-date material. However, it is critical to assess how quickly your selected platform enables for content updates.

All of this implies that you should carefully examine the training platform you are using, since this will affect the amount of time you have to spend updating the training content as needed. ensuring that employees receive the most up-to-date and accurate information is essential. Making training accessible to everybody It goes without saying that if we want to attain 100% compliance, the training must be available to everyone. Employees with visual or hearing impairments, as well as learning disabilities, are included.

However, it must also be inclusive, which is something different. Allowing learners to see instances of themselves in the text is one way to make training more inclusive. Employees are not all heterosexual, white, single males or females, nor are they all able-bodied. Training should be inclusive by 2025. It all comes back to the significance of engaging individuals by making it personal.

Compliance has an impact on businesses of all sizes. It is the compliance officer's responsibility to ensure that acceptable behaviours are known and ingrained in the business culture. This is more vital than ever in an increasingly regulated society. LMSs assist Compliance Officers in their pursuit of 100% compliance. This, however, is only half of the tale. You can only achieve 100% compliance if all sta - not just 90% or 95% - participate in the training and are supported to behave appropriately. This can only be accomplished by personalising and relevant training to not just your organisation as a whole, but to the position of each employee in the firm. It is also critical to ensure that you have the proper training materials in place to adapt to developing situations, and that all content is correct, up-to-date, and relevant.

Are organisations today actually putting employee loyalty first?

Employee loyalty is a mental congruence between the self and the organisation—a transformation from mere compliance to commitment. According to experts, when it comes to rewarding employee loyalty, devotion and the desire to go the extra mile are essential criteria. In the era of the "Great Resignation," where organisations strive to keep their star performers and professionals seek the next great opportunity, one of the concerns that has tormented us is, "What is the incentive for loyalty?"

This simple question sent us on a mission to grasp the enigmatic idea of loyalty—for businesses, leaders, and workers—and comprehend what it means to various individuals, if it should be rewarded, and whether enterprises are doing enough in this area. As new training demands and priorities develop, rms must be prepared with suitable training programmes to keep their sta up.

Leaders have become accustomed to constantly changing compliance norms and regulations; nevertheless, COVID has expedited change in ways no one could have predicted. For many businesses, the transition to remote work has added a layer of complexity that necessitates rethinking and overhauling workplace rules, procedures, and processes, as well as technology and perks, to meet the demands of a remote or hybrid workforce.

Another issue that organisations must address is digital harassment, and employees must realise that anti-discrimination and anti-harassment rules apply when working from home. Employees and applicants desire more family-friendly benefits that help working parents and caregivers, as well as EAPs, services for mental health and wellness, and employee appreciation programmes. Work-life balance is critical to the overall performance of workers and organisations.

It all comes down to workplace culture, which has grown in importance for both candidates and workers. People are curious about the type of firm for which they work. What are its ideals and principles, and how do they manifest themselves in specific, significant ways?We understand that in order to prosper, employees need to feel a sense of belonging and inclusion.

Make certain that supervisors provide regular, powerful messages to their direct subordinates about what constitutes excellent ethical behavior. Managers frequently overestimate the efficacy of compliance messages sent to their teams. For example, a manager may believe that proclaiming an "open-door policy" is the proper thing to do, but they fail to do anything constructive to invite or welcome a delicate topic. Managers should be reminded of their effect on employee behaviour, and compliance leaders should encourage them to demonstrate consistency between what they say and what they do.

Nonetheless, it was fascinating to observe that 35% of respondents ranked tenure as the second most essential criteria. As a result, while dedication and going the extra mile are the key determining criteria of loyalty, longevity also plays a role in this calculation. This is hardly unexpected given that most organisations continue to organise award ceremonies for their "long service" or "long tenure" workers, signalling that in reality, this is the most important criteria in determining tenure. Organisations invest enormous amounts of money on employee engagement and experience development, yet somewhere along the road, our approach has become far too generic.

Why do we paint employee engagement with a monochromatic brush stroke when we hire at an individual level and manage departures at an individual level?

If dedication and going above and beyond demonstrate devotion toan organisation, doesn't the inverse also apply? We, as an employer, are also committing to an employee, but are we going above and beyond to make that person happy? To understand what we can achieve, we must first understand what motivates people to stay loyal. Employee loyalty is ultimately driven by people and culture. With so much emphasis on the presence of loyalty, it was equally critical to discover its cause. Nearly 60% of our thought leaders identified "people and culture" as the most important contribution from a given set of statements, whereas 0% chose the "Human Resources Department." This emphasises that genuine exchanges and encounters, rather than predefined engagement activities, have an influence on commitment. This statement is reinforced by the fact that approximately 27% of respondents claimed that the "reporting manager" inspires loyalty since he/she/they are in charge of setting the tone on a daily basis. As we all know, "people leave managers, not organisations," and experiences are shaped by who one deals with on a regular basis, far more than the company's executive team or culture.

Modern training experiences should be customised to the needs of the enterprise. This involves properly explaining behavioural standards as well as defining pertinent policies, laws, and regulations so that workers can make the best decisions and businesses may avoid infractions, penalties, fines, and reputational harm. Furthermore, training may assist organisations in creating more courteous, inviting, and inclusive workplaces.

Reward positive conduct in a visible way. Many compliance programmes recognise the need to penalise individuals who demonstrate negative behaviours, but they frequently miss the equally crucial task of acknowledging positive actions within the organisation. Create situations in which small teams and groups of employees may collaborate on beneficial ethical practices. Sharing stories about employees who are doing the right thing not only inspires them to keep up the excellent job but also drives others to do the same. While there is still much work to be done, it should be heartening to compliance leaders that the greatest cultural solution is within their grasp. Companies that develop their cultures may begin to build a strong culture of integrity that will benefit their enterprises substantially in the future.

"Your business will not have a positive atmosphere if employees just know how to prevent wrongdoing."

This is crucial: organisations with strong cultures beat companies with weaker cultures in terms of both financial and nonfinancial goals. In powerful cultures: Employees are 90% less likely to witness wrongdoing. Employees who see wrongdoing are 1.5 times more likely to report it. Employees are more than twice as likely to be involved with their job and organisation and nearly 2.5 times more likely to put in extra effort. CEOs should assist employees in showing good conduct, ensure management transmits consistent signals, and make colleagues' positive behaviour more visible in order to promote an organisation's ethical culture.

"A 'no' uttered from deepest conviction is better and greater than a 'yes' merely uttered to please, or what is worse, to avoid trouble." – and "You must be the change you wish to see in the world." – Mahatma Gandhi

There are various everyday steps you can take to successfully detect and, more significantly, discourage ethical concerns in business from developing in your firm. When making decisions, be sure to express and enforce a strong code of ethics, and expect your workers to do the same. Maintain an awareness of the anti-discrimination legislation in your area. Keep up-to-date on the rules that affect your business, and make sure your organisation is following them. Work with accountants to ensure that your financial reports are transparent and honest. Be present in your organisation, ensuring that your organisation and its people are constantly doing the correct and ethical thing.

Creating an organisation culture in which workers feel safe raising their voices about everything from sexual harassment to sentiments of being insulted is a clear message for organisations and ethics and compliance authorities. This allows your compliance programme to address concerns before they become scandals, preserving the integrity of your organisation's culture internally and its reputation internationally. And never, ever accept retribution.

Poor corporate governance can lead to conflicts of interest, expropriation, and discrimination against minority shareholders. Small shareholders with little effect on the stock price are swept aside to create room for the interests of majority shareholders and the executive board. It has the potential to undermine public trust and taint society as a whole.

A lack of corporate governance may result in economic loss, corruption, and a damaged image, not only for the company, but for society as a whole, or even worse, for the entire world. This type of corporate governance is also intended to reduce risk and eliminate corrosive components insidean organisation. Corporate governance makes businesses more responsible and transparent to investors, and it equips them with the tools they need to address genuine stakeholder concerns, including long-term environmental and social development. Increased access to finance promotes new investments, boosts economic growth, and creates job possibilities, all of which contribute to development.

Avoiding ethical concerns inan organisation always begins at the top. Transparency and ethical company practises may be ensured by providing clearly established policies and processes that guarantee such policies are both acknowledged and adhered to.

As previously established, ethics and compliance are inextricably linked. In general, compliance is more effective in lowering risks when there is a strong ethical culture in place, and in the absence of a compliance programme, those who actively strive to violate laws and norms of behaviour can cause chaos. Strong cultures are defined by two factors: a high degree of agreement on what is valued and a high level of fervour about those values.

In the end, what happens to the top achievers who break the rules sends the most powerful message to the organisation. Whistleblowers will get a new voice as regulatory scrutiny grows, and the voice of the whistleblower grows stronger as well. Before going public, corporations must listen to and resolve the concerns of whistleblowers.

Managing culture and free speech in the workplace amid polarising times continues to focus on race, gender, sex, sexual orientation, gender identity, national origin, and religion—as well as people's rights to fair treatment, protection, and the rights and benefits of other. As privacy rules and the settings they govern develop, chief compliance officers are becoming increasingly concerned about data privacy. It is necessary to provide a safe and courteous workplace. As traditional networking models give way to online networks that provide new and unprecedented opportunities to exchange ideas and interact, the role of the compliance professional evolves and innovates.

From a large accounting fraud case in Germany to deceptive consumer techniques among Chinese-based corporations to unethical environmental activities in the United States, there is a long list of ethics and compliance failures in the business world. Your company's excellent name and stakeholder trust are two of its most valuable assets. By fostering an environment in which ethical behaviour is the standard, you can safeguard your company's reputation while also increasing employee engagement. Take the following methods to reduce your ethical risk:

- Assess your requirements and resources honestly.

- Create a solid foundation.
- Create an integrity-driven culture from the top down.
- Maintain a "values focus" in all situations, big and small.
- As required, re-evaluate and revise.

A good strategy is the foundation of any successful business. So, too, do effective ethics and compliance initiatives. To design a relevant and meaningful plan, you must first understand the terrain. Your program can only be effective if you start with an accurate assessment of your current strengths and areas of weakness. Your internal efforts should begin with risk assessment, followed by gap analysis and program evaluation. Audit reports are also an important component of the puzzle.

Your internal assessment to comprehend the situation on the ground:

- It is critical to understand that what ethical issues arise frequently in our work?
- Where are our most vulnerable points?
- Which ethical and compliance materials will be most beneficial to employees?
- What kind of assistance is most likely to be used and beneficial?
- What groups‘ input is needed for the development of our code and values?
- Which employees groups, locations, business divisions, and so on constitute possible hot spots?
- What are the values that our organisation and its workers hold dear?
- What values are required for our business, and particularly for our work?
- Who may be of assistance?

There are several methods for gathering information. Focus groups give a deep, rich picture of the status of ethics in your company by allowing a representative sampling of the greater community to express their ideas and experiences. Surveys (internal or done by a third party) allow you to collect information from a much broader group of your workers, compare findings, and analyse data by relevant subgroups (employees levels, departments, and units, for example). Start with ethical leadership at all levels of management if you're looking for a solution to the recurring challenge of how to foster an environment of trust, responsibility, and respect in the workplace.

Once you've identified your needs, you can put the tools in place to solve them by developing a strong ethics and compliance program. The good news is that such a program has an impact. The Ethics Research Center (ERC), the research arm of ECI, demonstrated as part of the 2011 National Business Ethics Survey that an ethics and compliance program is a powerful tool for reducing pressure to compromise standards and observations of misconduct; increasing employee reporting of observed misconduct; and decreasing retaliation against whistleblowers. In short, when a corporation invests in ethics, it makes a difference. Fewer employees feel pushed to breach the rules, and fewer wrongdoings occur. When improper behaviour occurs, employees notify management so the problem can be addressed internally.

Employees need to know that they can trust management to be honest and straightforward with them today more than ever before, since ambiguity breeds worry and dread. It's also a chance to develop a strong ethical culture that may support a business's future survival since employees will be glad to work foran organisation that cares about them and has their back. These feelings must not be suppressed or disregarded, but rather recognizesd in order to create a secure environment. If properly implemented, employees will go above and beyond the call of duty to guarantee that you all get through this together.

Organisations now operate in such a dynamic and competitive environment that you must adapt on a regular basis. Most change programs, on the other hand, fail to provide the desired results, and people's attitudes are a major contributor. Some people may welcome change because they see it as an opportunity to gain advantages and advance in the company; others, on the other hand, see it as a risk and have negative attitudes toward it.

In the latter case, people are thought to be resistant to change. This resistance might be due to their inability to adapt their behaviour, abilities, or dedication in order to fulfil the new standards; they may lack skills associated with change preparedness. People have a natural urge to fit in and adhere to the conventions of those around them, even after they have graduated from high school. Although it may be difficult to acknowledge, most people's ethical standards are very adaptable. Although most individuals want to "do the right thing," the idea of the right is often impacted by who they associate with.

Fortunately, a strong ethical culture is significantly more likely to develop if your firm has painstakingly created an ethics and compliance program and integrated it into the everyday operations of the corporation. According to research, a good ethics and compliance program contributes to the development of a culture of Integrity in which everyone "walks the talk." Employees at all levels are dedicated to doing what is right and respecting principles and standards in an organisation with a strong ethical culture.

Quality procedures must be championed throughout business, with leaders benchmarking successful organisations, implementing quality innovations, and establishing standards and measures in every area. Your ethics and compliance program must be a fundamental, integrated component of your job and the way you do it, ensuring that workers understand how to respect ethical and compliance standards in their work and feel supported in their efforts. Maintain established rules for ethical workplace behaviour as well as standardised training that provides information on ethical and compliance issues. A successful ethical and compliance programme will include the following characteristics:

- The ability to criticise management without fear of repercussions.
- Rewards for adhering to ethical norms.
- Not incentivising questionable behavior, even if it is illegal.
- Not encouraging problematic behaviors, even if they are beneficial to the organisation.
- Positive feedback for ethical behaviour.
- Employee preparation to handle wrongdoing and employees' openness to seeking ethics guidance.
- A method for reporting possible infractions in confidence or anonymously.
- Conduct performance assessments.
- Discipline systems for offenders discuss the significance of ethics.
- Keep employees up-to-date on problems that affect them.

- Keep pledges and obligations made to employees and stakeholders.
- Praise and recognise ethical behaviour.
- Hold people who break norms, particularly leaders, responsible.
- Exhibit ethical behaviour both professionally and individually.

Leaders are key corporate culture drivers; they set the tone in every firm. They select who gets seen, who gets promoted, and what deserves to be rewarded and recognised. They are the standard bearers. They serve as an example. Several actions should be taken by leaders to foster a strong moral culture. Character is everything.

Ethical leaders demonstrate integrity not just in their professional lives, but also in their personal relationships. In an age of social media, private conduct frequently becomes public information, affecting employees' perceptions of the kind of people their bosses are. While senior executives establish the tone for the business as a whole, supervisors influence the day-to-day conditions in which people work and make choices.

Supervisors' behaviour has a significant influence on employees' and their working behaviour. When a crisis occurs, leaders should realise not just the ethical dimension of the situation, but also the teachable moment it represents. Because of the depth of emotion involved, Edgar Schein, the pioneer of the study of corporate culture, observed that periods of crisis are particularly strong culture-builders. Employees learn a lot about their leaders' objectives and character when they display their true colors. Employees learn that ethics matter when leaders make values their touchstone in times of distress.

Ethics is about making decisions, both major and minor. Organisations with integrity maintain their ideals front and centre in both commonplace and exceptional situations. Corporate values should be included and expressed in a variety of procedures that drive the company's day-to-day operations, including:

- Human resource policies and their implementation.
- A system of rewards.
- Hiring and retaining employees.
- Management and assessment of performance.
- Decisions on promotions.

Situations and needs will shift. You must understand what is working, what isn't, what new vulnerabilities have appeared, how far you've come, and where there is still work to be done. Maintain a rigorous approach to reviewing the condition of ethics and compliance in your organisation on a frequent basis. Risk assessments, follow-up surveys, and regular or continuous focus groups will help you keep your program relevant while minimising risk. Regular assessments will also demonstrate internally that the resources you've invested in ethics and compliance have made an impact.

So, in the hope that any or all of this third batch can start a conversation or two, three, four, or five here on LinkedIn, in your workplace, or both, here is "round three" of my ethics and compliance conversation starters:

- If you think you can change the culture of your department or company overnight, you're setting yourself and your employees up for failure. I've seen it happen several times. Instead, conceive large, strategic concepts but then apply them in little, tactical, step-by-step, incremental activities. Sure, my concentration is on cultures that promote ethics, compliance, and accountability, but this strategy is essential for any type of culture change initiative. I guarantee it.

- If you're trying to market ethics training to your employees by telling them it would minimise their risk of ethical difficulties, stop. Simply put, quit. One of the few universals in business is that almost everyone, from the front lines to top management, feels they have nothing to worry about in terms of ethics. Someone else is constantly in need of attention. Yes, selling the concept of ethics training is crucial, but find another way.
- At its most basic, culture transformation is about ensuring that you are only promoting behaviours that are totally aligned with your values and objectives. It's a seemingly easy notion but, in practise, may be incredibly complex to execute.
- If you can't make an unarguable argument to your employees that ethics and compliance training are vital tools for their personal success, you'll constantly be "swimming upstream" to acquire their buy-in.
- If you're not sure how to do it, or even if you're doing it correctly, seek assistance. Outside eyes and ears may frequently see where you could be unwittingly supporting the sorts of behaviours you say you want to alter.
- If your ethics and compliance training aren't effectively integrated, you're missing a significant opportunity. You're missing the point if your ethics and compliance training are the same thing.

The lessons from scandals and organisational crises dating back to the early 2000s are clear: organisations are susceptible without an ethical and compliance culture. Strong cultures are defined by two characteristics: a high degree of agreement about what is valued and a high level of intensity about those values. In the long term, a strong culture of integrity serves as the foundation for a successful ethics and compliance program, which may provide a competitive advantage and serve as a significant organisational asset when properly integrated intoan organisation. Culture is increasingly becoming a defined, measurable, and improved idea, rather than a lofty, fuzzy one. Organisations may face a variety of hurdles in building a strong culture of integrity and an ethics program, but there are solutions to overcome these challenges: Organisations may face a variety of hurdles in building a strong culture of integrity and an ethics program, but there are solutions to overcome these challenges:

- Organisations can use employees surveys and independent observers to build listening posts, such as cultural evaluations, to acquire a more accurate picture.
- While senior leadership may work hard to develop an integrity culture at headquarters, policies and communications might get lost in translation as one goes out of the central office.
- Culture must be actively and continuously addressed, especially in big enterprises with remote outposts.
- Employee turnover may also harm an organisation's culture. Organisations now must appeal to the biggest multigenerational workforce in history.
- To build cultures that last, organisations should promote an atmosphere that combines a "something for

everyone" appeal with a set of consistent principles that all generations can accept. Internal disputes are resolved fairly at all levels of the company. I observe that employees may not always agree with outcomes, but they are more likely to accept them if they think the process was properly handled.

- Cultural fit is one of the most difficult challenges in integrating a merged or acquired firm; in fact, it is one of the reasons such deals fail, despite the potential commercial benefits. As part of the due diligence process, executives may wish to undertake a cultural audit.
- If the values of the target firm differ greatly from those of the buyer, this might be a warning indicator. A well-thought-out integration strategy can assist both organisations in understanding and reinforcing desirable values.
- An organisation is a group of individuals who share common interests and beliefs and work together to achieve a common objective.
- Creating a culture of integrity not only fortifies the business against risk, but it also fosters employee engagement and strong affiliations with all stakeholders.
- Nothing can wreak havoc on culture more than the naysayers. They can stymie the organisation's operations by causing barriers. They should be recognised, coached, and given the opportunity to conform to anticipated conduct, or they should be removed from the organisation.
- The business hires and screens people based on both character and skill. The onboarding process instils corporate values in new workers, and mentoring reflects those principles. When employees depart or retire, they

are treated with dignity.

- The organisation recognizes and promotes employees in part based on their commitment to ethical standards. It is obvious that good conduct is rewarded, but it is also evident that poor behaviour, such as attaining outcomes regardless of technique, may have negative effects.
- Operational directions and business imperatives are consistent with leadership messaging about ethics and compliance. Front-line and mid-level managers put ideals into action. They frequently employ the power of stories and symbols to encourage ethical conduct.
- Many businesses are taking calculative steps to strengthen their code of conduct and related controls and processes, as well as to promote accountability for ethical behaviour through training and performance evaluations.
- Reward appropriate conduct while penalising inappropriate behaviour. Don't take sides. Leaders frequently fail to express their beliefs and expectations. More is preferable in this scenario.
- Conduct cultural evaluations to get to the heart of how individuals behave and think.
- Maintain a positive attitude in the middle: Much depends on middle management's ability to translate top-down tone into rules and procedures that drive day-to-day conduct.
- While many employees avoid discussing ethical issues for the reasons stated above, many others do so out of fear of reprisal. This may be solved by anonymous ethics reporting, in which anybody withinan organisation can voice their ethical concerns while remaining accountable.

- A compliant workplace not only helps to recruit fresh talent, increase performance, and strengthen employee morale, but it also adds toan organisation's overall success.
- Find new and imaginative ways to transmit cultural values and to recognise and reward values-based behaviour. To encourage people to relate their stories in order to bring their values to life.
- After determining an organisation's existing ethical situation, communicating the code with workers, and developing an ethical position with visible top leadership buy-in, a targeted ethicalisation process must be implemented through the following organisation-wide practises.
- Using ethical hiring strategies in recruitment and selection means employing people who have strong ethical principles and emphasising ethics while hiring new employees.
- Providing ethical training; emphasising the importance of strict adherence to the code of Ethics; ensuring that the lessons learned are applied in the workplace; discussing ethical issues with new hires as part of their onboarding process; communicating core values to newcomers and others (core values serve as long-term guiding principles that must be repeatedly repeated through training, corporate videos, and public meetings to change behavior).
- Rewarding ethical behaviour; evaluating procedures as well as outcomes; avoiding a bottom-line mindset; measuring ethical behaviour; disciplining workers who break ethical norms.
- Raising Concerns and Protecting Whistleblowers by assisting employees in raising concerns when something

goes wrong; creating an environment in which workers feel comfortable speaking up and addressing ethical concerns;Establishing a rigorous framework to protect the interests of whistleblowers.

- Holding workers responsible for their activities; accepting responsibility for one's own actions and effects.
- Taking ethical considerations into account when making decisions and discussing ethical issues at meetings.

In current times, I've seen this strategy used to inflate the figures of an organisation trying to be purchased, desperate for venture capital money, under pressure from shareholders, or just motivated to have the numbers booked. This technique does not appreciate the consumer, does not provide a great experience, and does not establish a relationship. Customers suffer, as do workers who were motivated by unethical behaviour. Believe me when I say that if you take advantage of a customer's vulnerabilities, they will ultimately catch on, and an ex-customer with a grudge is a liability; they'll be ready to share negative experiences and the identities of shady salesmen. We've all spent time assisting a potential customer to come up to speed, only to have them opt to do business with someone else. It's never a nice feeling to lose a sale, but you may take solace in knowing you made your best competitive effort. Time has proven that for every prospect who is handled with care and educated thoroughly, trust and goodwill are built.

That trust may not pay off immediately, but it is a sensible investment in the long run. Things may not go as planned with the rival, and the prospect may return to you. Alternatively, they may consider you for follow-up work or their future employment. Sales stars differentiate themselves by nurturing client connections. You are creating something lasting by improving your understanding of clients, anticipating their wants, listening to their criticism and suggestions, and rewarding them for their loyalty. Too frequently, ethics are depicted as purely personal.

However, this way of thinking allows corporations to get away with unethical activities or deceptive rules. You set the tone as leaders. Those on the path to creating (or keeping) a trusted brand do so by incorporating strong ethics and values into their company strategy, including C-suite decision-making, sales methods, and HR rules. Unnecessary service contracts are never offered by trusted brands. It is their commitment to integrity, sustainability, governance, and community. "Congratulations to Kimberly-Clark for being named one of the world's most ethical companies."

Ethisphere names Kimberly-Clark One of the World's Most Ethical Companies for 2022: "Kimberly-Clark has always been devoted to conducting business the right way," stated Mike Hsu, Chairman and CEO of Kimberly-Clark. "We are thrilled to be recognised by Ethisphere once again; it reflects the profound dedication of our employees throughout the world to lead with integrity as we push our value creation agenda for all of our stakeholders." Kimberly-Clark is one of just four winners in the consumer products sector. Ethisphere will celebrate 136 awardees from 22 countries and 45 sectors in 2022. The World's Most Ethical Companies assessment process, which is based on Ethisphere's proprietary Ethics Quotient®, includes more than 200 questions on culture, environmental and social practises, ethics and compliance activities, governance, diversity, and initiatives to support a strong value chain. The process provides an operational framework for businesses across sectors and throughout the world to gather and codify best practises.

"Today, corporate leaders confront their most important mandate yet: to be ethical, accountable, and trustworthy in order to achieve good change."-Timothy Erblich

Career advancement is proven to be an important component in attracting employees. Businesses must consider ESG as a business strategy, not just a compliance requirement. Consumers, and even workers, nowadays are discriminating and feel required to patronise organisations that they perceive to be socially responsible, ecologically conscientious, and financially viable. Along with bolstering CSR programmes, how can today's leaders instil the correct values at the organisational level? Greaves Cotton has always prioritised reskilling and job readiness for persons from poor communities. To usher in such initiatives, the corporation must first meet all legal requirements, make environmentally friendly business decisions, and put in place effective systems to maintain good governance standards. It is critical that we recognise that industrial plants seldom survive without community support and engagement. Businesses would benefit from cultivating this relationship based on mutual trust and respect. How can organisations avoid falling into the trap of tokenism while promoting ecologically and socially conscious activities among employees and in company operations?

To escape this trap, consider doing good as a strategic objective for an organisation's long-term success. There must be a minimal gap between what the organisation says about itself and how the rest of the world views it. When this happens, trust in the brand skyrockets and businesses prosper.Again, this is contingent on businesses doing the right thing, whether in the realm of ethical business practises or ecologically sustainable operations. One thing that comes to mind is whether or not loyalty can be purchased. Is it necessary to build it through people's cultures? Can it be determined during the hiring process? Do we believe that if an employee's career is unstable, he or she will be untrustworthy? Can loyalty be viewed differently from the employer's perspective? And how may this be made distinctive foran organisation?

Antiquated incentive systems that included gold watches and employee pension plans at the conclusion of an employee's career have given way to more relevant incentives and perks provided throughout the employee's tenure with the company. Many executives responded to our poll with novel ideas for loyalty awards! Appreciating direct family members of the employee, one-on-one encounters with the leadership team, choosing an "Employee of the Decade" who shares his/her/their experience with the firm, social media gratitude, and more were all popular themes. Giving the employee a new advisory position in the firm, offering greater career possibilities, increasing responsibility and involvement in future-oriented initiatives, providing avenues to upskill and upgrade, and even building a particular career progression plan based on their objectives were all prominent themes. Another intriguing incentive suggestion was to learn about the employee's personal interests or social concerns and sponsor one of these ideas to help them realise their ambitions! This would go a long way toward making the employee a committed advocate of the firm since they would have felt really cherished and exceptional.

Employee loyalty is a mental alignment between oneself and one's employer—a path from compliance to commitment. According to experts, when it comes to rewarding employee loyalty, devotion and the desire to go the extra mile are essential criteria. In the era of the "Great Resignation," where organisations strive to keep their star performers and professionals seek the next great opportunity, one of the concerns that has tormented us is, "What is the incentive for loyalty?"

This simple question sent us on a mission to grasp the enigmatic idea of loyalty - for businesses, leaders, and workers - and comprehend what it means to various individuals, if it should be rewarded, and whether enterprises are doing enough in this area. Our first stop on our market research journey was introspection, looking at our own experiences as employees and employers. We tracked the situations in which we saw loyalty, and we realised that, in the eyes of the beholder, loyalty is evident when it exists, crystal plain when it does not, but it is also practically hard to define when it rests in the grey region.

Unfortunately, the majority of people fall within the grey region. So, how do we define loyalty? Is it a fiction of our mind, an ethereal sensation, or an objectively anchored product of something?For us, loyalty is influenced by three factors: the leader's vision, the entire environment in which we operate, and organisational culture. Having said that, we know that loyalty is difficult to measure when workforces contain a variety of generations - baby boomers, Gen Z, and Gen Y all coexisting, each with a unique perspective and loyalty metric.

Furthermore, today's workplace is different; it no longer relates to a physical office where upward mobility is as visible as the C-suite on the top floor. A one-size-fits-all approach to loyalty will not work in this day and age.To better understand the concepts of loyalty, we sought out to roughly 40 CXOs, top academics, and other industry thought leaders to assist us in developing an educated perspective on the matter. This exchange is summarised in the sections below.

In today's business, defining employee loyalty via mindset alignment. Whatever your response, it goes without saying that recognising loyalty is just as vital as any other type of monetary award. Devoted workers understand the business, concentrate on their work, are rarely absent, and are less alienated and more devoted. This is why loyalty will continue to be a key value for many organisations: it brings tangible commercial benefits.

Finally, little or large acts of appreciation can have a significant influence on an employee's faith and trust in the business. It demonstrates that we are paying attention and caring. And this creates a really human system of recognition and rewards—one that engages, motivates, and develops the talent we have worked so hard to develop.

"Corporate governance can ensure lasting and reliable commercial performance, regardless of the type of endeavour. A lack of corporate governance may result in economic loss, corruption, and a damaged image. Proper corporate governance is no longer only about investor protection; it is now a must for organisations to prosper."

-Dr. Amit Das

About The Author

Dr. Amit Das, is a renowned executive advisor, consultant, educationist, author, speaker, counsellor, and coach whose 25+ years of business experience provides high-impact, practical solutions that support his clients' leadership development and organisational transformations. He worked for fortune 500 company and left rich leagacy of organising transformational learning workshops. He has transformed more than 5000+ working executives through his path breaking capability building learning workshops. Dr. Amit Das is recognised as an innovative, principled thought leader who combines intellectual rigor and discipline with an ability to translate theory into practice. His operational skills are coupled with a strategic ability to analyse, develop, and implement successful strategies for profitability, growth, and sustainability.

Dr. Amit Das has a successful track record in aligning learning and training solutions to key business strategy with a strong focus on flawless execution excellence to facilitate individual, business divisional, and organisational performance. He keeps relentless focus on measuring training impact and ROI, people capability building graphs, training process governance, performance coaching, and strategic thinking. These have been some of his key individual success traits. His core capabilities include performance coaching, designing training and development frameworks, psychometric assessment and analysis, competency framework development and assessments, content design and facilitation of soft skills and leadership programmes, Learning Management Systems, Learning Impact Measurement, Talent Analysis, and Performance Coaching and Counselling.

Dr. Amit Das has authored multiple management and self-development books, like High-Impact Leadership, Redefining Corporate Spectrum, Create Your Leadership Edge, Love-Laugh- Live With Happiness, SMART Parenting @ Zero Cost, Redefining HRM, Building Organisational Capability, Ethical Road Map, Attomic Attention, BYPB, Redefining The Power Of Mentoring, Making The Most Future Fit Organisation, Redefining Talent Management, Defining Your Success Factors, Lead or Plead, Make The Most Of Your Life, Better Half or Bitter Half, Psychology Of Learning And Development, The Transformative Mind & Soul are few of them.

He has a Ph.D. and a Fellowship in strategic learning, along with his first class degrees in Human Resource Management, Marketing Management, International Business, and Corporate Laws from the top business schools in India. He is a certified Psychometric analyst, HR Analyst, OD Interventionist, Human Psychologist, Lifecoach, Leadership Developer, Black Belt (LSS), Strategic Thinker, Talent Analyst, certified professional trainer from the U.K. and certified behavioral coach from the U.S.A.

Dr. Amit Das likes googling, reading books, writing articles & books, cooking, listening to old melodies, and counselling people to unleash their true potential to build a strong nation. He is married and blessed with a son. He would love to hear about your experience after reading his books. You can email him and share your thoughts, or you can use his services for life coaching, positive behavioural counseling, educational support, and mentoring for young, promising students pursuing their B.B.A. and M.B.A. degrees.

References

- *Business Ethics, Faith That Works by Larry Ruddell, 2014*
- *Global Business Ethics by Ronald Francis, 2015*
- *Bad Pharma How drug companies mislead doctors and harm patients, 2014*
- *Conscious Leadership by John Mackey, Steve Mcintosh, Carter Phipps, 2020*
- *Business Ethics lessoned Learned by Richard m Bowen, Niki Nicastro McCuistion, 2017*
- *Ethics For Managers by Joseph Gilbert, 2016*
- *Believe In People by Charles G Koch, Brian Hooks, 2020*
- *Business Ethics by Stephen M Byars, Kurt Stanberry, 2018*
- *Social Entrepreneurship and Business Ethics Understanding the Contribution and Normative Ambivalence of Purpose-driven Venturing by Anica Zeyen, Markus Beckmann, 2018*
- *The Rise Of Business Ethics by Bernard Mees, 2019*
- *Issues in Business Ethics and Corporate Social Responsibility by Sage Researchers, 2020*
- *Business Ethics A Philosophical and Behavioral Approach by Christian A Conrad, Denica Webb, 2019*
- *Strategy, Law and Etyhics for Business Decisions by Christine Ladwig, George Siedel, 2020*
- *Business Ethics Now by Andrew Ghillyer, 2017*
- *Corporate Social Responsibility by Andreas Rasche, Mette Morsing, Jeremy Moon, 2017*
- *Business Ethics by Alejo Jose G Sison, 2018*
- *Understanding Business Ethics by Peter A Stanwick, Sarah D Stanwick, 2015*
- *A contemporary Look at Business Ethics by Ronald R Sims,*

2017

- *Business Sustainability, Corporate Governance, and Organisational Ethics by Zabihollah Rezaee, Timothy Fogarty, 2019*
- *The Business Guide to Effective Compliance and Ethics Why Compliance isn't Working - and How to Fix it by Andrew Hayward, Tony Osborn, Thomas Hickey, 2019*
- *Business Ethics, Contemporary Issues and Cases by Richard A Spinello, 2019*
- *Business and Professional Ethics by Leonard J Brooks, Paul Dunn, 2020*
- *Intentional Integrity: How Smart Companies Can Lead an Ethical Revolution by Robert Chestnut, 2020*
- *Governance, Risk Management & Compliance by Richard Steinberg, 2020*
- *The Business Guide to Effective Compliance & Ethics by Hayward & Osborn, 2020*
- *The Business Guide to Effective Compliance and Ethics: Why Compliance isn't Working - and How to Fix it by Andrew Hayward and Tony Osborn, 2019*
- *Corporate Risks and Leadership: What Every Executive Should Know About Risks, Ethics, Compliance, and*
- *Human Resources by Eduardo Esteban Mariscotti, 2021*
- *Peng, M. (2016). Bundle: Global Business; Bundle: Global Business, Loose-Leaf Version, 4th + MindTap Management (Ch6. 6-6c Benefits and Costs of FDI to Home Countries).*
- *Feloni, R (2018, November 14). GM CEO Mary Barra said the recall crisis of 2014 forever changed her leadership style. Business Insider.*
- *James, J (2020, February 25). General Motors named one of the 2020 World's Most Ethical Companies by The Ethisphere Institute.*
- *Gapper et al (2020, January 19). What Japan Inc Really*

Thinks About Carlos Ghosn, Nissan's Maverick Savior.

- *Ciulla, J., & Solomon, R. (2018). Chapter 12: When the Buck Stops Here: Leadership. Honest Work A Business Ethics Reader (4th ed). NY: Oxford University Press.*
- *The Remix, How to Lead and Succeed in the Multigenrational Workplace by Lindsey Pollak, 2019*
- *The Ethics Of Money Production by Jorg Guido Hulsmann, 2018*
- *Business Ethics, The Search for Elusive Idea by Todd Pheifer, 2017*
- *Unleashing Capacity, The Hiddeen Human Resources by Rita Trehan, 2016*
- *Business Ethics, An Ethical Decision –Making Approach by Mark S Schwartz, 2017*
- *Ayn Rand and Business Ethics by Stephen Hicks, 2019*
- *A Good Life In The Market by Gary Chartier, 2019*
- *Business Ethics Case Studdies and Selected Readings by Marianne M Jennings, 2017*
- *Business Law, The Ethical, Global,and E-Commerce Environment by Arien Langvardt, A james Barnes, Jamie darin Prenkert, Martin A McCrory, 2018*
- *Ethics in Information Technology, George Reynolds, 2018*
- *Law and Ethics In The Business Environment by Terry Halbert, Elaine Ingulli, 2017*
- *Business Ethics Mindtap management by O C Fereel, John Fraedrich, Ferrell, 2018*
- *Business Ethics best practices for Designing and Managing Ethical Organisations by Denis Collins, 2018*
- *Business Ethics Managing Corporate Citizenship and Sustainability in the Age of Globalization by Andrew Crane, Dirk Matten, Sarah Glozer, Laura Spence, 2019*
- *The Power Of And, Responsible Business Without Trade-Offs by R Edward Freeman, Bidhan l Parmar, Kirsten*

Martin, 2020

- *Resisting Corporate Corruption by Stephen v Arbogast, 2017*
- *Markets, ethics, and Business Ethics by Steven Scalet, 2018*
- *Managing Business Ethics by Linda K Trevino, 2017*
- *Business Ethics For Better Behavior by Jason Brennan, William English, John Hasnas, Jaworski, 2021*
- *Business Ethics In Action by Domenec Mele, 2019*
- *Organisational Ethics by Craig E. Johnson, 2021*
- *Managing Business Ethics by Alfred A Marcus, Timothy J Hargrave, 2020*
- *Business Ethics by William H Shaw, 2016*
- *Business Ethics Decision Making for Personal Integrity & Social Responsibility by Laura Hartman, Joseph DesJardins, Chris MacDonald, 2020*
- *Business Ethics Moral Principles That Govern the Conduct of Businesses by Razaq Adekunle, 2020*
- *This is Business Ethics by Tobey Scharding, 2018*

www.ingramcontent.com/pod-product-compliance
Ingram Content Group UK Ltd.
Pitfield, Milton Keynes, MK11 3LW, UK
UKHW040005200726
13854UKWH00001B/46

9 798888 692400